HOW TO ACE AN INTERVIEW

Job Interview Preparation, Interview Questions and Answers YOU Need to Stand Out and Get Hired

Liability/Warranty

HOW TO ACE AN INTERVIEW

Job Interview Preparation, Interview Questions and Answers YOU Need to Stand Out and Get Hired

ROBERT MOMENT

CONTENTS

INTRODUCTION

"A job interview is NOT just a two-way conversation; it's a strategy to get hired."
Robert Moment
The Get Hired Expert

You prepared an excellent resume and an equally superb cover letter. Congratulations! Your interview has been scheduled and, of course, you are overjoyed. However, you begin to experience a mild panic attack, what can you do to ace the interview? In the current job market, you have already made great progress by landing an interview. Take a moment to pat yourself on the back and then get to work. You now need to carefully and thoroughly prepare for your interview. The better prepared you are, the more self-confidence you will project during your interview. The significance of the interview cannot be overstated; the interview is your time to shine, and you owe it to yourself to adequately prepare for your big day.

Sure the resume you labored over for months got you noticed, but that's only half the battle. You still have to close the deal by acing the interview process, and beating out the competition. However, have no fear. With preparation, and the job interview tips and strategies in this book, you can win over your prospective employer.

Getting a job, is just like getting a date, getting a sales appointment, or getting anything that requires someone to make a considered - or rash - decision as the case may be - and as hard as getting that date or appointment may be, it's even harder to follow-up and optimize the opportunity. That is, what happens now when you get that date or job interview? You've got to follow-through on the initial enticing premise that got you the date or appointment in the first place. After all, your 'target' has been 'pre-sold,' your job is to keep them sold and close the deal.

At the job interview, it is very important that you convey to the interviewer *your value* to their company; this is one aspect the interviewer will be investigating during the process of the interview. Emphasize your physical appearance, level of confidence and interpersonal skills. When you are preparing for an interview you should take into account all these factors and act accordingly.

Get hired interviewing better than 99% of job candidates.

If you want to ace a job interview, prepare yourself right from the beginning. This book is written to help you master all the technical aspects of an interview. You will find out:

- How to Prepare for a Job Interview (ideas, tips, strategies)
- Soft Skills You Must Have to Stand Out and Impress Hiring Managers

- Tips and Strategies for Acing a Job Interview
- 100 Interview Questions and Answers You Need to Ace to Get Hired
- How to Turn an Interview into a Job Offer
- How to Create a 30-60-90 Day Employment Action Plan That Will Impress Any Hiring Manager
- Tips and Strategies on How to Successfully Close an Interview and Follow-Up.

This book will give you the job interview tips, ideas, and strategies you need to answer the #1 question on the mind of every hiring manager:

"What problem would hiring you solve?"
(Why Should We Hire You?)

Ace your job interviews and
get hired for the jobs you want!

CHAPTER 1
HOW TO PREPARE
FOR A JOB INTERVIEW

"The ability to sell your knowledge, skills and talent is your strongest asset in a job interview"
Robert Moment

A job interview is a big deal. You need to impress the interviewer in order to get the job; this is the main reason why you should do everything possible to properly prepare for your job interview. This means dressing appropriately, grooming yourself properly as well as practicing your speaking voice. Grooming is a very important factor in job interviews.

When going on a job interview, it is very important to go through proper interview preparations; to stand out from other candidates who are not as prepared. Having trouble answering questions and appearing that you are simply not ready can destroy any chances you have of being offered the job pretty quickly. Therefore, it's important to hone your interview skills; one way to do this is by practicing. In this chapter, we will discuss various interview preparation tasks you should engage in prior to going on a job interview.

The first thing you need to do is read the job description closely; this will let you know exactly what the company is looking for. You then need to tailor your professional and personal strengths, experiences and skills to the job. The first opportunity you have to do this is your cover letter. Make sure that you mention how your experience and working background fit the skill set required for the job. Tailor your resume, to the job requirements, so that it appears that you are perfectly qualified for the job.

You also need to find out all of the information you can about the hiring employer. Find out how long the company has been in business, what they sell, what services they provide to the community, who is their target market, and what's going on in their industry. These are all things that you should know prior to going into the interview so that you can speak intelligently about the company, their needs and what they are facing. Employers want these types of individual's working for them because they are invested in the job and are interested and know enough to contribute to improving the company.

Another interview preparation tactic is to know exactly where the interview site is, showing up late for an interview can severely hurt your chances. Therefore, you may want to do a MapQuest or drive out to the interview site prior to your interview. Also make sure you leave plenty of time to actually get to the interview in case you get lost.

Having strong interview skills is important to being able to land a job. While you won't be able to know ahead of time exactly what questions the interviewer may ask you, there are some common questions you should be prepared to answer. Also, it is important to know yourself, your strengths, your weaknesses, what you want out of your career as well as being knowledgeable about the company; if you prepare yourself with this information, you'll be able to answer almost any question intelligently.

Be prepared to answer questions about your past experiences, how you have dealt with difficult situations and how you have worked alongside other people, and give examples. Many companies are utilizing experienced based interview techniques to get a better idea of what type of candidate you are. Here are tips to help you prepare:

Tip #1 - Research - Most companies now have websites that provide a wealth of information about their background. Take it a step further and try to find the company on social media outlets such as Facebook, Twitter, and/or LinkedIn. The night before your interview, spend 20-30 minutes researching the company's history, mission, news releases, culture, promotions, products, and services. The interviewer will be impressed that you took the time to learn about them.

Tip #2 - Know Your Resume - Study your resume and know it inside and out. There's nothing worse than not knowing what's written on your resume and having to constantly stare at your resume for answers. You wrote your resume so you should know it well!

Tip #3 - Dress to Impress - Don't wait until the last minute to find something to wear. I've seen dozens of candidates come to interviews wearing a shirt so wrinkled that it looked like it was rolled up in a ball. Additionally, as I mentioned under Tip #1, know the company's culture. Don't wear a suit if you're going to interview with an action sports or surf company. At the same time, don't wear shorts & sandals if you're going to interview with a financial services firm.

Tip #4 - Sell yourself - Remember you are the best candidate to sell yourself, to any prospective employer. You understand your weaknesses and strengths best. Focus on that one thing in your personality, previous job experiences, and educational background that sets you apart from the rest. It is normal to feel nervous and jittery about expressing all these things before a panel; therefore, take time to build your confidence level by practicing what you will say. Groom yourself well, because when you look good you feel good.

Tip #5 - Timeliness - You can never have a second first impression. Don't show up late to a job interview, if you live in a city where traffic is heavy, leave early! If you live in a city with inclement weather, leave early! Regardless of whether you have GPS in your car, print a hard copy of the directions in case your GPS dies on you. If you have time, the day before your interview, drive by the interview location. That way, you limit any risk of difficulty finding the location the day of your interview.

I've seen people show up late to an interview and boy did they look frazzled!

Tip #6 - Understand the position in the company – When preparing for any job interview, it is critical to understand the type of position you are interviewing for, entry-level or more experienced. If it is a more experienced position, the interviewer will focus on your educational background, personality, and previous work experience. The employer is trying to determine how your educational background, personality and previous experience has contributed to your achievements in your previous position and how these skills will benefit them if they hire you. It is vital to have a clear understanding on how to answer interview questions for the type of position you have chosen.

Tip #7 - Role Play - It may sound corny, but role playing an interview is like rehearsing before a play or musical. You can easily find a list of interview questions in Chapter 8 and give them to a family member, friend, or significant other. Have the person ask you the questions and role play the interview with them. You'll find that on the day of your interview, the answers will come to mind with ease!

Tip #8- Create the Perfect Elevator Pitch- Write a simple, concise, compelling and memorable elevator pitch that will answer these three questions (Who are you? What do you do? What do you want?). When the interviewer asks you the question- "Tell me about yourself." Practice your elevator pitch and be confident in selling your skills, talents, experience, and value you will add to the employer.

Strategies to Get the Job You Want

Practice, refine, practice some more. Think of the many celebrities and politicians you've seen interviewed, no doubt they have been well prepared. Practice will enable you to quickly answer the interviewer's questions without being caught off guard. You'll also be able to convey the information you most want the interviewer to know about you.

Have a brief summary of your professional past in mind. Most of the questions will likely be about your past work experience. Be prepared to discuss your responsibilities at jobs you held with other companies. Open-ended questions like "Tell me about yourself," are designed to elicit responses about your professional background moreso than your personal attributes.

If you have any gaps in your employment, you may be asked to explain them, present your situation in a positive light. Clarify how you used the time productively and kept your skills up to date during that time away from work.

Focus on the positive. When answering, be honest, but present yourself in your best light. Expound on your successes and accomplishments, but don't ramble, if you can provide specific examples to illustrate your points, do so, but only give one or two. More than that will bore the interviewer.

Express confidence, not arrogance. Yes, it's a fine line to walk. At a job interview you're expected to toot your own horn. After all, if you don't tell the interviewer about your accomplishments, he won't get a true picture of who you are. Ideally, you should be able to support your claims with facts.

For example, if you say that you're a good salesman, provide some figures that prove your abilities. Perhaps you increased sales at your last company by 10% or you were responsible for $3 million in sales the past year; those are pretty compelling facts certainly worth sharing.

Be straightforward about your weaknesses. If asked about your weaknesses, don't deny having them. However, rather than focus on your problem areas, explain how you are taking steps to overcome those issues. If you're someone who doesn't like to delegate, explain how you're learning to identify tasks that can be passed to others to increase team productivity.

Choose your words carefully when talking about your past. In describing previous jobs and employers, resist the temptation to badmouth. While your feelings may be justified, you won't seem professional if you speak negatively. Instead be tactful and diplomatic. Explain career moves in terms of your plans to grow and learn.

Smile as you speak. A pleasant expression will make you appear to be relaxed. Besides, nobody likes a grouch. Be a good listener. An interview should be a conversation in which both parties participate. If you want to establish a rapport with the interviewer, you'll need to appear interested in what he's saying, make good eye contact. Let him finish his thoughts before speaking. Stay focused on answering the specific questions he's asking.

Ask questions. You should also be prepared to ask some questions of your own about the company and the responsibilities of the position you're applying for. Your interest will be noted and you'll also have more information to use in deciding if this is the right job for you. Be a natural, but professional version of your true self. You want to be memorable, in a good way. As in a social situation, you should be polite, nice, and likable.

Preparing For a Job Interview Both Mentally and Emotionally

Preparing for a Job Interview: The Mental Preparation

Let's face it! There is lots of competition out there in the job market today. Not only do you need to be prepared for the questions you may get asked but you also need to be emotionally prepared. If you are nervous or lacking confidence, then the interviewer may not have a lot of confidence in your either. Mentally prepare for those questions by rehearsing your answers beforehand while thinking about how they may be received by the interviewer and prepare yourself emotionally by doing some relaxation exercises. Some common questions include:

- What do you know about the company?
- What are your strengths?
- What are your weaknesses?
- Why did you leave your last job?

Preparing for a Job Interview: The Emotional Preparation

If you are very nervous going to the interview, it might help to realize that everyone has a certain amount of anxiety about interviewing. A little bit of nervousness is good; it gives you energy! If you are tremendously nervous, you will want to focus on your breathing. People, who suffer anxiety attacks, have very restricted breathing. They breathe at the top of their chest in shallow breaths, rather than down to their belly. See if you can open your chest and take a few slow deep breaths and let the air travel right down to your abdomen. Focus on relaxing each part of your body, starting from your feet all the way up to the top of your head. By merely bringing your focus to your breath and consciously relaxing your muscles, you will begin to feel more calm and centered. You might also want to close your eyes (but not if you're driving) and take a few minutes to visualize a successful outcome to the interview. Imagine yourself as calm and poised during the interview, imagine the interviewer smiling and shaking your hand afterwards telling you what a pleasure it was to meet with you. Remember that practice makes perfect and if you do not succeed at getting an offer on the first round of interviews, chalk it up to practice and you will eventually be successful.

Six Major Insights You Gain by Visiting Your Interview Site the Day Before

1. You will learn about the company dress code. Visiting the interview site is especially critical because you'll learn a bit more about the company culture. It will give you an idea of how to dress for the interview. You will also know how you can expect to dress at the company once you are hired.

2. You'll be well aware of how long it really takes to get there. It is easy to underestimate how long the commute will be from your home to the interview site. Many job seekers now have GPS navigation systems that help take the guesswork out. If you don't have access to one, consider borrowing one from a friend. However, even if you have one, you must remember that the estimated time of arrival is only an estimate. It depends on the speed you travel, the number of stops along the way, and the traffic pattern. Also keep in mind that you must make sure your

GPS maps are up to date as some newer locations may not show up on your map. If you don't have a GPS, consider what you would do if new construction begins the day before or the day of your interview? What if the route you were planning to take is closed for unforeseen circumstances? It is better to be sure than guess the length of the commute.

3. You'll know of any major traffic jams. Always visit the interview site at the same time that you expect to leave the next day. In doing so, you can be sure you are aware of any major traffic concerns that may pop up during certain hours of the day on various routes.

4. You'll get an idea of what the parking situation will be like the next day. Nothing is worse than getting to the interview site on time and then realizing that you have to pay for parking and you don't have the money. Even worse is when you realize that the place you will park is already packed with cars and finding a spot will be a nightmare. If you go the day before you can get a feel for what you will face the next day. As a result, you will be much calmer!

5. You'll know the locations of gas stations, and convenience stores. The unexpected can happen at any time. You may run out of gas unknowingly. If you are a woman, you may find you have a rip in your stocking. You may need to pick up gum or mints because you forgot them at home. Anything can happen! It is smart to know where you can stop on your route in case you forgot something. Always know your options!

6. You may discover a new route. During your dry run, you may find a new route that will get you to the interview much faster; this is wise because even if you run into a traffic jam, you will know what other ways you can take to get there.

CHAPTER 2
HOW TO HOLD ATTENTION, BUILD RAPPORT AND CONTROL A JOB INTERVIEW

No matter how many interviews you have gone to it never really seems to gets easier, does it? That's because each interview is different. Each interviewer is different from the last one and often the position you are applying for, although in your field of expertise, is different even if only slightly.

However, there are ways you can feel more relaxed and controlled in interviews, and increase your chances of getting that job or promotion.

Here are ten tips to help you approach a job interview more confidently to increase your chances of success. The tips don't appear in any particular order as everyone needs to improve in different areas, but there is something here to help everyone who has ever been nervous about a job interview.

Treat each interview as special
Approach each job interview as a new experience that requires you to sell yourself and your skills differently. An interview is about finding out if you are a good fit for a job, do not try to repeat answers you rehearsed months ago for another job.

Being well prepared for each interview will help minimize your stress and increase your chances of landing that perfect job.

Do your homework
Part of interview preparation is in knowing something about the company. It also means knowing at least the name and the position of the person who will be interviewing you.

As part of your interview preparation, familiarize yourself with the job description of the position. If you don't already know this information you can get it by going to the company's website or by making a phone call to their human resources department.

There is one question every interviewer asks during the interview, that question is:

"Why do you want to work for this company?"
The question may not be asked exactly like this, but something like it will be asked. If you have researched the company it will be much easier to answer questions like this without having to figure it out at the last minute and you'll also feel more confident.

Make time for job interview practice
Once you have the information concerning the company and the job position you are applying for you can develop some anticipatory practice questions you might

think you will be asked in the actual interview. After making a list of these questions you can then begin practicing answering them in front of a mirror or in a mock interview.

Ask a friend or family member to help you with the mock interview. Also, many school career centers are a great resource for interview help. Your local library may have employment videos that you can check out and watch from the convenience of your home.

The point is to take advantage of as many resources as possible to help you sharpen your interview skills.

Dress the part
The day before your interview select the clothing you are going to wear. As you prepare for your interview, make sure your attire is appropriate for the company.

Men should wear a nice pair of slacks with a dress shirt and tie, sport coat or a suit. Women can wear either a skirt or slacks with a dress blouse.

Both men and women should not dress provocatively or outlandishly, or with an excessive amount of jewelry. If you are going to wear jewelry keep it simple.

Take what you need to the interview
You will want to bring copies of your resume to give to the interviewer, even if you submitted one with your

application. Your resume should be neat, clean, and professional looking.

Also, take along a pen and pad of paper to take notes. Doing these things demonstrates your sincere interest in obtaining the position.

Be punctual

Make every possible effort to arrive at your interview on time, in fact, be there a little early, never be late.

If you show up late for your interview, you have told the employer that you are not punctual and will be late to work. If you are going to be late you need to have a very good reason, and call the employer to explain the reason in advance to find out if you can reschedule the interview.

Stay calm

During the interview stay calm and answer questions in an even and friendly tone of voice, expressing what you know about the company and how your skills can enhance and benefit the company.

Make eye contact with the interviewer when she is speaking, this will demonstrate your interest in what she is saying. Never let your eyes wander around the room as this will show a lack of interest in not only the position, but the interviewer as well.

Sit comfortably

You don't want to slouch in the chair at your interview, but you do need to be comfortable. Try and sit up straight, and take a few deep breaths. This posture will not only make you look calm and in control; it will help to make you feel this way too.

Ask questions

You don't give over all control in an interview: at least, you shouldn't! An interview should also be about finding out whether you want to work within the company. It may seem quite a different place once you are there, so you want to find out what the place is really like.

Also, asking questions will impress the interviewer. It will make you appear interested and intelligent and also willing to learn and listen to people. Realizing that you also have the right to ask questions at your interview should help you stay calm.

Closing the interview

When the interviewer brings the interview to a close let her know that you appreciate having received the interview and restate your interest in the position. Leave the interviewer with a positive impression of you, and you will feel that reflected back at you.

You will feel much happier as you leave the interview room.

These are tried and tested ways to approach a job interview more comfortably. If you prepare for your interview thoroughly, and remember that your world will not end if you don't get this job, and that you have the right to refuse the job, even if it is offered to you, you should feel much better about going through the interview process.

Be calm, friendly and open. The interview is not a threat to you. There will be other jobs if you don't get this one and it may not be the best fit for you.

Approach a job interview in a detached and rational manner; showing less emotions will help you feel calm, and do well on your interview.

Taking Control of a Job Interview

Imagine the poor job interviewer. They sit at a desk talking to one boring job applicant after another. The page of questions before them is full of unintelligible notes and maybe the occasional doodle. What can you do to entertain this person?

Can it really take that much? Look at them! They want to be entertained. They want to find the right job candidate. They want you to be the right person for the job.

You can't bring your puppy into the interview to entertain them. Sure, that would get you noticed, but it probably wouldn't get you the job.

Think about the industry of the position. What is the most exciting part of any industry or subject? It's the new stuff; it's the things that are written about in trade magazines and blogs. That's what your interviewer will talk about in the hallway between interviews, the cutting edge stuff is what interests them.

Do you know cutting edge industry information? Do you know the job? Share your knowledge with the interviewer.

Take control of the interview. Talk about current events of that industry. It will not be hard to work that into the conversation. Moreover, it will get the attention of the interviewer.

You may wonder what happens if the interviewer is strictly an administrative type that isn't up to date on their own industry. That doesn't matter. If you are passionate about the industry, the interviewer will know. After all, they hear that kind of talk every day from their coworkers. They will tell the people they work with that you sound like the rest of the people in the company.

Take control of the job interview as soon as you can. Ask the interviewer questions. Talk about the industry, show your passion. The interviewer will not care and will not ask about your biggest weakness, so you'll avoid that question. If you want it, you will get the job.

Why do job interviews cause people to panic?

A pending job interview can cause a person to experience a variety of physical and mental symptoms. However, the question is why? Why do people freak out when having to be interviewed? There are a number of reasons but after doing a bit of research and thinking about my own past experiences, I've listed the top five.

1. Fear of exposure and lack of confidence.

Everyone experiences fear at some point in time and most people encounter situations where their confidence is tested, people who fear being interviewed are dealing with something deeper. An interview can be a very intimate dissection of ones professional anatomy. People who are shy or introverted will feel the pressure even more. Suddenly they are the center of attention and must open up to a total stranger.

Interview questions can get personal because employers realize they are getting a whole person. For example, a person who has been unemployed due to a family issue might have to touch upon the gap in their employment history. A person who is dealing with confidence issues will feel a heightened sense of awareness of every little insecurity and inconsistency.

2. Lack of preparation

When you go to an interview without any preparation, you are leaving your fate to the wind. I realize that some interviews can occur on the spot; however, most people are given a window of opportunity to prepare. So, why don't people properly prepare for interviews? Well, some people don't know how. While others do not think it is important or necessary. The average person will go days and even a week before even thinking about the interview. Then the day before, they will print out copies of their resume, iron their clothes and call it a day. Doing the prep work can be the difference between having a successful interview and realizing you are at the wrong building, and your interview was an hour ago across town.

3. Exaggerated accomplishments or avoidance of questions

Some people feel anxious and even fearful because they have not been forthcoming on their employment application. They get to the interview and hear the distant chant of "liar, liar, pants on fire." However, why do people lie? I personally believe that people lie for a variety of reasons, and if it's the job of their dreams, they might feel that they cannot afford to let this chance slip away. People lie because they feel the employer won't understand their circumstances. These days, job applications are usually straightforward. They want to know if you have what it takes to do the job. What positions have you held? Have you ever been convicted of a crime?

If you did not do it, you cannot claim it. We might call it exaggerating, but it's lying when you claim to have held a job or accomplished a task when you did not. There is nothing wrong with putting your best foot forward. However, please do not lie. With technology, background checks, and so many resources, your employer can find out the truth. Remember, people have been hired and then fired because of lying on a job application or during an interview.

4. Unrealistic expectations

Unrealistic expectations can cause a person to become anxious. A person's expectations consist of the ideas and views that create a perceived outcome. Having a realistic view of your situation, the job, your experience and your objectives can help alleviate many concerns and give you a proper perspective. For example, you are interviewing for an Executive Assistant position with a salary scale between $55,000 and $70,000. You are expecting to be offered something in the middle. You are offered $57,000 based on your three years of experience. Keeping realistic expectations are necessary when entering an interview before, during, and after.

5. Not really committed to the job

Everybody needs a job. However, finding a job you love is a challenge. If you interview and you are not really committed to doing your best or perhaps not really interested, it will show during the interview. Managers want employees who will bring, not only their skills, but an enthusiastic attitude to the workplace. Employers want your commitment; they want you to want to be a part of their company.

Let's face it, no one likes being scrutinized and judged; however, this is a part of a job interview. The interviewer must select the candidate she believes is the right fit. Each interviewer has a different set of criteria, so there is no 100% guarantee of the outcome. Even when you think you did your worse, you can get hired because the intervener saw something she liked such as your infectious smile or your can do attitude. Interviews go beyond what is written in your CV or resume; interviews even go beyond interviews.

Here are some additional tips to help you ease anxiety, and develop a winning attitude that will last long after the interview is over.

Tips for success before, during, and after the interview

1. Be prepared. Have the latest version of your resume or CV. Bring copies, if possible, and give yourself enough time to review your information. You might want to ask a friend or relative to help review the information with you, and ask you some questions.

2. Dress for success. Dress as professional as possible. Put yourself in your potential employer's shoes, would you hire you to represent the company? Like your mother always told you, mind your manners. It does not matter what environment you could be working in a first impression can go a long way.

3. Check your personal hygiene. When you are nervous, you perspire more. Brush your teeth, carry mints or gum but do not use excessive perfume or cologne. Comb your hair. If you have long braids or long hair, consider putting your hair up or tied back so your prospective employer can see your beautiful/handsome face.

4. If you get nervous or have dry mouth, consider carrying a bottle of water. Take a sip while you wait and then right before the interview.

5. If you are sitting with other candidates waiting to be interviewed, do not be alarmed. Stay focused on yourself. Do not worry about how the other candidates look, what they are wearing or what they might say. Do not, I repeat, don't you dare compare yourself to someone else. If you engage in a friendly conversation, keep it light. Remember, it is okay to focus on yourself and not engage in a lengthy conversation with other candidates.

6. Be honest about your experience and job duties. Do not exaggerate what you can or cannot do. If you have been convicted of a crime, your interview is the perfect chance for you to elaborate on the circumstances. Be honest about your past jobs and your roles. Remember, people have been fired from a job because of lying. You do not want to ruin your reputation or future chances with the company.

7. Remember, panelists are people too. Chances are your hiring manager or panelists have sat where you are sit-

ting. Remember, you were chosen to be here. You got the call so you must be doing something right.

8. Keep your mind focused on the positive things that you have to offer. Think of at least two or three positive things about yourself. If you cannot think of any, remember, you are a hard worker and you want a chance to do something you love. You are not like everyone else; you have something unique to share with the company. You have earned the right to be here, you belong in the interview and you have nothing more to prove.

9. Please, don't put much into facial expressions. People make faces all the time. You don't know what is going on with the interview. She could be having a horrible day, gas, and hunger pains. People put on poker faces to hide many different things and they are not always negative.

10. Give yourself some credit, remember you are also conducting an interview. These are the people with whom you could be working. When given a chance to ask questions, ask the interview why she chose her career or why she chose to work for the company.

11. Take a deep breathe before you respond to each question. Do not rush or force an answer. Listen thoroughly and respond carefully. Take notes and do not be afraid to ask for the question to be repeated or elaborated upon.

12. Be yourself. If you had an English accent when you arrived, please have it when you leave. Seriously, be honest, be fair, and be professional.

13. Say thank you. Remember to always thank the panelist or interviewer for their time and the opportunity.

14. If you didn't get the job, try it again. Practice, practice, practice. Apply for another job, make notes about what worked during your last interview and where you could be stronger. If you can record yourself while a friend or family member does a mock interview, that can help you review your tone, body language, and responses.

15. Building confidence. Confidence is one of those things that can be developed. As long as you do your homework, you are more than good enough and deserve to be where you want to be. Remember employers can pick up on how you feel about yourself even when you think you are hiding your feelings.

Finally, did you know that no one can control how you feel and what you do? You are not the first person to get nervous, make a mistake, or question your choices. However, you are the only person who can take control and choose to have peace of mind before, during, and after the interview.

CHAPTER 3
INTERVIEW SKILLS THAT
WILL GET YOU HIRED

Understand that your curriculum vitae or resume is meaningless if you cannot sell your talents, skills, and abilities to hiring managers.

Your resume or CV does not guarantee you a job. Do not think your great degree will guarantee you the job. There will be others with higher degrees and grade point averages applying for the same job. You want utilize effective interview skills that will make you stand out with hiring managers by highlighting your talents, skills and abilities.

Do not get lost in Human Resources

Human Resources personnel organizes, sorts and files resumes. Your objective is to get your resume in front of the hiring manager. When creating your list of contacts, focus on managers; they are the ones that will conduct the interview. Making the right contact before the interview will help your attitude at the interview. You won't be sitting in front of a new face. Your nerves can then be at rest.

Understand that the real match making takes place before the interview

In your job hunt, make every effort to ensure that you are a good fit. Know the parameters of the job when you walk into the interview. Research the company, find out about its culture, goal and competitors. Familiarize yourself with the company before you go to your interview. Be mindful that some corporations have dress culture, and some have company colors. Packaging yourself to suit the culture of the company gives you an edge. If you are serious about getting the job, research the company. Perform a thorough examination of the profile, work-culture, turnovers and history of the company. Knowing everything about the company will be useful in your interview, and will help you decide if you would like to work for the company. Additionally, interviewers like an applicant who has sound knowledge about the company. Your interviewer will easily detect from your speech that you have done your home work. One of the best ways to learn about a company is to talk to people who work there. Take initiative, network with people who are where you want to be.

Focus on accomplishments

Employers use behavioral interview strategies to leverage past performance to predict a candidate's future potential. The employment selection process is as challenging for employers, as it is for potential hires. Acing behavioral interviews is not as difficult as it appears, showcasing past accomplishments is a powerful antidote to challenging behavioral interview questions and can catapult an ordinary candidate to the "most promising" shortlist.

Remember the employer wants to hire you

A company holds interviews so it can find the best person for the job. The hiring manager will be ecstatic if that person turns out to be you because then he or she can stop interviewing and get back to work. Give yourself an attitude adjustment, convince yourself that the manager wants to hire you, doing this will help you have a positive attitude in the interview and may influence the hiring manager to feel good about you.

Pretend the interview is your first day at work

Most people treat an interview as though it is an interrogation. The employer asks questions and the candidate gives answers. Your attitude should be that of an employee who is there to talk about a new project rather than the more obsequious attitude of a candidate hoping to get an offer.

Keep some answers ready

Be prepared with answers to some classic questions like:

- What are your strengths?
- What are your future plans?
- Why do you want to join this company?
- Are you a team player?
- Why should we hire you?

Substantiate your answers to these questions with actual situations and solid resolutions, use real life experiences to prove your point.

Practice your interview answers

Practicing for your interview can be the most effective step toward landing your next job. If you have a video camera or cell phone, have a spouse or friend record your practice interview. Pay close attention to your body language and tone. Also be prepared to answer both common and behavioral questions and limit your response to one or two minutes.

Learning how to properly answer interview questions can help you stand out above the competition and improve your chances of getting hired.

Ask questions

It's a good practice to ask questions, generally 5-6, at the end of the interview. Asking questions shows the interviewer that you are interested in the company and the position as a whole.

Be prepared

Prepare, ahead of time, for your interview. Review your resume and be prepared to explain how your experience and skills align with the position. Research the company prior to your interview; review the company's website and other publications to learn as much as you can.

Plan to arrive at least 15 minutes prior to your interview; use this time to focus on your breathing to relax and stay calm, this will help you easily answer interview questions and feel confident about your responses.

CHAPTER 4
WHAT EMPLOYER'S WANT TO HEAR
IN TODAY'S COMPETITIVE JOB MARKET

The most important thing that an employer wants to know is how you can contribute and bring value to their business; this is a universal rule, regardless of what you do, and where you are.

A question that you might want to ask yourself is: Do I care about the employer?

While you're getting ready for your interview, a lot of questions are swirling around in your head:

- Do I look good (Image is Everything)?
- Will I make a good impression?
- Can I answer the interview questions correctly?
- Are they going to like me?
- Do I have enough experience?
- What kind of job offer will they make?
- Is my salary going to be better than my previous job?
- How do I negotiate my desired salary?

If you take a good look at the questions, you'll see that they're all about you! Yes, you think about yourself and you care about yourself more than your potential employer.

It is natural for a person to think and fend for themselves. However, from an employer's perspective, this does not look good. You need to shift your focus to your prospective employer.

- What do they need?
- What do they want from their employees?
- What are their current company problems? Man-power, management, process?
- What are their primary concerns?
- How can I be an asset to the company?

So, what do they want to hear?

A hiring manager wants to know that a candidate can perform the job duties; however, this is not the entire reason for employing someone, hiring manager's look for a candidate who can solve an existing problem they have. They want to hear answers to their problems, they want to know how you will be an asset to their company.

For instance, the interviewer has a problem, they have a vacant position and they need to fill it. However, they don't just need an individual to do a specific job, they need someone who is going to solve their problem, they need someone who is going to take responsibility for the role and remove the responsibility from the interviewer.

A job or a role is not just about fulfilling a job description, it's about taking responsibility for the job. If the you can demonstrate that you will be responsible for the position it is easy to establish your ability to perform the role in question.

Even if someone is not completely qualified, the interviewer would rather train a candidate who is willing to accept responsibility than hire someone who is more qualified but does not appear to be willing to accept responsibility for the job.

How many times have you heard someone say "I am completely qualified for that role I should get it"? Well, as demonstrated above there are other factors that come into play when securing a role through the interview process. The ability to perform the job is one aspect, demonstrating that you will take responsibility for the job shows that you can more than meet the interviewers expectations for the role; you may not be the perfect fit for the role, but you demonstrate key elements the interviewer either consciously or subconsciously desires.

Recognize that the employer is looking for a candidate who can fill a specific need and contribute to the success of the company. The interviewer will not take the time to connect the dots, and assume because you did a function well that it will translate into performing well in an allied function.

Moreover, these needs differ from company to company and certainly from industry to industry. Your answers to interview questions should, as often as possible, demonstrate that you are the only candidate that can fill the employer's needs. Prepare for your interview by getting the basic information down, and building in the necessary flexibility to effectively answer questions.

As a general rule a job interview consists of a buyer (the employer) and the seller (you). If you are selling what the buyer wants to buy the possibility of success goes way up. Give solid examples of how you resolved challenges that the employer is facing; this is what successful candidates do in job interviews, give the interviewer strong assurances that you can do the job. Why, because you effectively performed identical functions in the past and there is a high likelihood you will do the same in the future. Copy this model and you will be successful in your job hunt.

By placing focus on the needs of the employer, you can increase your chance of getting the job; by doing so, you will be less nervous and less afraid during the interview. Look at yourself as an actor who is trying to overcome stage fright. Actors learn to overcome their fears by focusing on their audience rather than themselves. Think more about your audience (the interviewer), and your stage fright will diminish.

CHAPTER 5
SOFT SKILLS YOU MUST HAVE TO STAND OUT AND IMPRESS HIRING MANAGERS

In a job interview you have the chance to accomplish your dream of getting the job you want; by preparing for your interview you are getting closer to realizing your dream. It is important to be able to think like an employer, so that you can say what your interviewer wants to hear, what he wants to be done, and act the way he (or she) likes.

When you are interviewing for a competitive job opening, you need to know how to make yourself stand out during the interview process.

Your soft skills can help you stand out and impress hiring managers. Soft Skills can be defined as the set of communication habits, personality traits, charm, and positive behaviors that come into play when an individual interacts with another person. One might fall into the trap of thinking that soft skills can only be applicable in jobs such as sales where person to person interaction is key, but this is not true. If an IT technician can effectively communicate with other business units within a company then the productivity within that company will increase significantly, and that particular technician will be viewed in higher regard.

Training courses for such skills are increasingly being offered to aid individual's to improve themselves and allow them to perform their jobs better. Examples of such training courses can be Power Speaking, Implementing Change, and Memory Empowerment to name a few. Moreover, while these may be a few of the more popular examples of soft skills, various others qualify - such as being flexible, adaptability to change, creative thinking, and tolerance to cultural diversity. You may innately possess some of these soft skills.

Of course, soft skills are by no means the sole deciding factor that employers base their hiring process on, but they go a long way to impress a hiring manager.

So what crucial soft skills do you need - those under-taught skills that will make the difference between getting and keeping that job.

Time management – time management has far more to do with managing yourself rather than your time. If success depends on effective action, then that action is your ability to focus your attention where it's needed most and not responding solely on how you feel in the moment. Multiple demands and many distractions can be challenging, you're going to have to get used to shifting your focus - you do it all the time flitting from Facebook to work project to text to web surfing in a matter of minutes. Being "busy" doesn't equate to being productive and effective!

Communication - Think about how you come across to others. Empathy is a key skill you need to actively nurture both on and off-line. Your presentation skills must be meticulous for any interview - that's a threshold requirement. You need confidence to project yourself, speak honestly about your strengths and weaknesses and communicate with passion and integrity.

Good communication skills are in big demand in any career, yet employers often cite these as lacking in the workplace, which is a little surprising, since we all communicate with other people on a daily basis.

However, we communicate with different people in different ways and knowing the appropriate forms of communication in a work environment is what matters when it comes to finding a job.

Young people use abbreviations when texting or emailing each other, which is fine, but becomes a problem if they don't know how to spell and construct sentences properly as well as understanding text-speak.

So, if you are good at spelling and have a decent grasp of basic grammar you are at an advantage in the job market. Moreover, if you can't spell and haven't got a clue about grammar, don't despair - it's not too difficult to learn. You will find everything you need free online, all you have to do is perform a simple search. Or if you prefer to use a book, you'll find plenty of resources at your local library. Fifteen to twenty minutes a day should soon get your written communication up to speed.

Networking - How good are you at this skill? We live in a world dominated by constant information exchange and daily innovation. Your relationships are your only competitive advantage and they create the channel through which ideas and information flow, where new ideas are shared, discussed and perfected. If you can cultivate a large relationship network you will meet the right people, find that job, build a business, learn about new trends, and share ideas.

Writing - A lost skill and one that might not have been taught properly in the first place. Shocking but true. You absolutely have to be able to write proficiently so that others can understand you. Writing well includes everything from emails, cover letters, and a CV, write clearly, directly and intelligently. Use your writing skills to take notes - one of the most productive things you can do because they'll help you remember what you see, hear or read when you're learning something new or trying to remember something specific.

Optimism - You may think that how you act is a product of how you are feeling, but you will find that you can change the way you are feeling by how you act. A great attitude always leads to great experiences. Moreover, you're going to need that great attitude no matter what life throws at you. You've got to be able to generate and radiate goodwill to maintain a competitive edge. Optimism can be learned.

Critical Thinking - Every day you're bombarded with large amounts of rapidly changing information. You need to be able to evaluate it, sort the valuable from the trivial, analyze its relevance and meaning and relate it to other information relatively quickly. Without this ability and awareness of thinking sharply, you'll be left behind. You've got to be able to challenge assumptions, look at things from lots of different angles, think outside the box, collaborate with others and be solutions-focused.

Personality

This depends on the job. You might be required to be a team player to fit in a group that is already working, or you might be required to have leadership and management skills if you are going to supervise that group. Whatever the personality required for the job you'll need to show, both with words and your behavior, to the interviewer that you have these skills.

Adaptability

Being able to adapt to changing circumstances, emergencies and any of the other unpredictable events which occur in the workplace is a critical skill in the current climate.

These soft skills are also transferable skills, there is a strong likelihood that you will be able to draw upon many of your life experiences if you have not used them in the workplace. Be sure to demonstrate these skills, it will boost your chances of getting the job after the interview.

People Skills

This covers quite a broad range and includes the ability to get along with people from all walks of life and to work in a team and take instructions from your supervisors. Interpersonal skills are gained in just about every part of life from school and college to work and social occasions. These are transferable skills, if you don't have much work experience, you should have plenty of examples to call upon.

Creativity And Problem-Solving Skills

The ability to apply both logic and creativity to solve problems is highly valued by employers. If you are the kind of person who tries to see the solution as well as the problem, this will help you stand out in the interview.

Examples of Soft Skill Questions

1. After my first couple of months here, I was assigned (whatever). I had never done this before and felt I didn't have the experience to do a good job at (and on and on and on). Have you ever been in a similar situation? (Really asking: Are you the can-do- type?)

2. I don't usually bend the rules to get a job done. Have you ever broken the rules? (Trick question:

Can you think outside the box to solve a problem?)

3. I'm an introvert/extrovert. Do you work better alone or in a group? (Are you capable of teamwork?)

4. Our department is expected to meet deadlines. If your deadline is in one hour and a co-worker is having problems with the copier, what would you do? (The real question is would you spend a couple of minutes to help your co-worker?)

5. Sometimes our department does not get complete information from our corporate office. Has anything ever gone wrong because you didn't get all the information? (Really asking: Was your verbal/written communication skill the problem?). The most frequently used communication ability question is "Do you have any questions for me?"

Ways to Build Soft Skills

Employers want recent examples of your interpersonal skills. They don't usually care what you did more than one or two years ago. Providing recent examples of your interpersonal skills can be a challenge for new graduates and people who have been out of the workforce for extended periods of time. Luckily, there are many ways you can keep your talents up-to-date.

Learning something new demonstrates your can-do attitude and problem solving skills. Scanning job postings for "preferred" items can be your source of inspiration, you want a job, but you don't have certain requirements. First, you are proactive in learning the skills that the employer wants. Second, you have solved the problem of joblessness.

Volunteering is a noble way of building teamwork and service skills. Many organizations more than welcome volunteer expertise to help organize programs, contact donors, and assist with office work.

Showcase your creative problem-solving skills, teamwork, and service talents by starting a support group or action committee in your neighborhood. Do elderly neighbors need transportation for errands? Are children tripping on uneven sidewalks lining many of the streets? Identify a problem, form a group, find a solution, and solve the problem with results.

Writing is an excellent way to exercise your capacity for written communication. Start a blog or write for an online magazine in your area of expertise; doing this will give an employer easy access to samples of your writing style.

CHAPTER 6
THINGS HIRING MANAGERS LOOK FOR
IN JOB INTERVIEW CANDIDATES

There are a number of things for job seekers to consider when looking for work. However, it is important to be aware of what employers look for in each candidate. In a very competitive job market , candidates cannot underestimate the importance of understanding what it is employers are looking for.

Job Interviews are much like auditions, often it is the excellent performance that gets the gig. However, not everyone is cut out to provide a stellar performance in the pressure chamber of an interview. Even for the best candidates, a moment in the spotlight can give them a sense of stage fright.

The first lesson in nailing an interview is to know exactly what hiring managers look for in a candidate. Yes, there can be literally hundreds of details-from wardrobe choices to resume format-and a nervous applicant could get bogged down with any one of them. Keep in mind the old saying, "don't sweat the small stuff."

Stick to the basics and improve your chances of getting the job.

In preparing for a career-making audition, a few things should top the list. Ten things hiring managers really look for:

Attention to detail: This starts with your application and flows through to the work you will do. Having a keen eye for detail puts you ahead of the competition, and is particularly important when it comes to your resume and cover letter (which are your "first impression") with an employer.

Ability: Not surprisingly, the entire hiring process rests on this simple premise. Can the candidate do the job? In the excitement of making it this far in the hiring process-past the initial application, telephone screening, and resume submission-many candidates fail to ask themselves this fundamental question. Carefully examine the requirements of the position, this should be part of your preparation for the interview, and be prepared to explain how you can do the job. If you can't do the job, you won't get hired. Know yourself before you apply; this also means that you need to be aware of your skills relative to the job posting.

Education/Experience: These two elements are often used as qualifying factors to trim down the applicant list. This doesn't mean you can't get hired without the right mix, but you may face an uphill battle convincing the employer. Follow this rule, if you have 70% of the desired education and experience, you should apply to the job.

Initiative: Managers love employees with initiative. If you can anticipate what needs to be done (and start before being asked), you will be on your way towards a successful career; this is one of the most important traits candidates can have in the today's economy.

Communication Skills: This is often overlooked by candidates, but it appears on almost every job posting. Discovering that a candidate's written and verbal communications skills are lacking will often derail their application. Do your best to ensure your application package is as perfect as you can make it.

Good Fit: Every company has a way of doing business, beyond what is in the employee manual-commonly referred to as "corporate culture." If you are a leisurely person, then you might have difficulty in a formal suit-and-tie office. It is like forcing an oval peg into a round hole; it is close, but not enough to be a fit. For many job seekers, a casual atmosphere would be a welcome change of pace, just make sure you can perform in that environment. Again, researching the company prior to meeting with the hiring manager is critical to identifying its corporate culture; this is one of the intangible elements that can make all the difference. Hiring employees who fit the corporate culture makes the entire team more productive, it's difficult to evaluate fit before you are hired, but researching the company's culture can help set you apart.

Confidence: Confident people are more persuasive, more likely to take calculated risks, and can command the respect of those around them. These types of candidates make employers swoon. An effective resume tells a story-of past accomplishments, education, and strengths; it does not reveal who you are. The interview is an opportunity to rise above a piece of paper (or electronic file). If a resume is inflated, embellished or puffed-up, it will become apparent in a face-to-face meeting. In sales, the cardinal rule is "never overpromise and under deliver." The interview is exactly the same.

Studies have shown that potential for the future trumps past accomplishments when judging a candidate for a job. Expressing confidence and the sense of "the best is yet to come" could be enough to get a candidate over the top and into the position.

Trust: Skills and experience are the key traits in a new hire, but trust (or the lack of it) can be a quick deal breaker. Is a candidate trustworthy and believable? Hiring managers look for the right person they can depend on to perform the job functions, or conduct the business. Even the best jobs have complex, difficult or even mundane tasks; employees must be relied upon to fulfill those tasks, no matter what. Of course, it takes time to build the groundwork for trust, but in the interview, a first impression of trustworthiness is crucial-without it, your chances are zilch.

Team Player: Collaboration is a skill that is necessary; responsibility rarely rests on someone who cannot work

well with others. This also plays into the corporate cul-
ture-will a candidate's unique style overshadow the
expectations of the team or will their contribution ele-
vate the entire group? One may have a role in the office,
but without the support of others, it can create conflict
that could lead to problems.

Character and Sense of ethics: Another important
thing hiring managers look for is character and a strong
sense of ethics. Strong character coupled with professionalism determines your interpersonal skills. Your past
experiences and references of your former superiors are
critical aspects which typically impress recruiters.

Show these essential characteristics as a job candidate
and stand out with Hiring Managers.

CHAPTER 7
25 TIPS FOR ACING A JOB INTERVIEW

Job applicants spend a lot of time working on their resumes, and to a lesser extent, their cover letters in hopes of getting a job. However, in reality, resumes secure interviews not jobs. It is during the job interview that you will either make or break it. Here are 25 tips for acing your job interview.

Research the Company

When you go for the interview you should know everything there is to know about the prospective company. Employers want to know that you are interested in what they do. Gather all the information you can and be ready to answer questions like "what do you know about this company?" and "why do you want to work here?" You need to ensure you have fully researched the company you are looking to work for. Go on their website and find out what they do, where their locations are, and the number of employees. You don't need to know every little detail but a basic understanding will not go unnoticed by the interviewer. You can use the internet for this research but don't be afraid to call the company and ask for some information or literature.

Dress Professionally

You would think this would be a slam-dunk, and yet it is not. It should go without saying that you must wear your "best" business suit, it should be pressed and clean, and your shirt can be blue or white and your tie cannot be a conversation piece. Beyond that, you must have clean grooming with neatly trimmed fingernails. Your shoes must be clean and polished. The interviewer will begin to make her or his assessment of you within seconds of meeting you; their initial, blunt assessment must be positive.

First impressions matter when you go on a job interview. Make sure your clothes are neat, clean, and fit you correctly. You don't have to wear designer clothing to land a job, but you do need to be presentable. Ladies,wear a nice contemporary and professional outfit, make sure that you wear appropriate makeup and jewelry and have your hair clean and tidy. Men, make sure that your hair is combed and that any facial hair is neatly groomed. In general, flip flops are never appropriate for an interview, so make sure your shoes match your professional appearance.

Be Prepared

Not only should you have copies of your current resume with you; you should also have copies of any documents or evidence to support claims you will make about yourself. You may never hand these documents to your interviewer but having them handy and ready will do wonders for your confidence. Being able to reference and show your portfolio to your interviewer as the interview progresses will add weight to your credibility.

End Each Answer With a Question

You should speak no more than two minutes at the time. More important, after answering the interviewers question ask a related question back to the interviewer. Engage the interviewer in the process. Never put the interviewer on the spot which means you should be tossing softball questions at the interviewer. Still, softball does not mean irrelevant or simplistic. You must ask good questions without putting the interviewer on the spot. This goes back to being prepared, you should be well prepared with questions and insights. You must remember that an interview is a two-way street. There are a list of questions in Chapter 9 you can ask the interviewer that will make you stand out.

Ask For Follow-up

You must never leave an interview without asking for follow-up. If the interviewer does not give you a clear course of action, then it is up to you to offer a course of action. Regardless of who initiates the next step, you cannot leave without a clear understanding of what that next step is. If you do not, then you wasted 30 or 45 minutes of your life.

Speak Clearly and With Purpose

If you need to, take a short moment and think about what you want to say (not too long or it will become awkward) in order to avoid using fillers such as "mm" "um" or "hmm;" this will make your answers precise, purposeful, and clear.

Talk about yourself

Don't sell yourself short even though it may feel a little uncomfortable talking about yourself to a stranger. Speak about your qualifications in relation to the job, what skills do you have other than those specific to the role? What are your interests? Be personable and let the interviewer know you are alert and present in the conversation.

Body Language

Make sure that you look the interviewer in the eye. Don't fiddle or twitch as you sit. Sit up straight and look confident. Be well dressed and well groomed, you will never be looked down on for overdressing for an interview.

Be on time

Punctuality is very important for obvious reasons. If you are late to your interview then what is the employer going to think you may be like on the job. I would recommend either staying in a hotel the night before if the interview is not local. Alternatively you should give yourself an extra hour on whatever journey time you think you may need. Never be late for a job interview. Find out exactly where the office is located, so you can allow yourself time to get upstairs if your appointment is on the 30th floor of an office tower. If you are taking public transportation, allow enough time for unexpected delays. Giving yourself an extra window of time will allow you to arrive fresh, rather than stressed and worried about being late.

Develop your Profile

One of the best tips on acing the job interview is to put together a portfolio of your technical and personal qualities that will be beneficial to the employer. Make a mental portfolio, but feel free to write it down, just make sure you have it memorized for the interview. Your technical qualities should be those specifically related to the job requirements such as educational training, knowledge of software applications, past experience and so on. Your personal qualities are things like time management, communication skills, organization, and professionalism. Know your qualities inside and out and be ready to sell yourself.

Prepare and Practice

Preparation and practice are probably the best and easiest of the tips on acing a job interview, but the most overlooked. Get a friend to interview you, record yourself, and do whatever you can to prepare your answers. Be ready for a behavioral interview. They are more common now and you will need to think of specific times when you had to solve problems using the skills that you outlined in your profile. Prepare a few different scenarios that you have experienced and rehearse them. Also have some questions ready for the interviewer. Employers like to see that you are interested in them as well.

Be Ready to Positively Critique Yourself

It is almost a definite that an interviewer will ask you what your weaknesses are; this always throws everyone off because we are often so focused on selling ourselves to the employer and telling them how all of our strengths can benefit them, we get anxious when asked about our weaknesses. Have them ready. Don't go giving a long list of them (you still want to look good) but prepare a few and be ready to tell why they are your weaknesses. It doesn't end there, you must tell the interviewer what you are actively doing to remedy a particular weakness, this way you are turning what is a negative, into a positive. This leads into my next point; don't be negative! Please resist the urge to slander a former employer no matter how bad! Being negative never makes a potential candidate look good.

Know Your Strengths and Weaknesses

During any interview you will probably hear, "What is your greatest strength?" and its adversary "What is your greatest weakness?" Make sure you know how to answer these questions, think about your answer before the interview and have it ready to rocket out of your mouth when asked. You do not want to hesitate telling them what your strengths are, this shows integrity of your words and exudes confidence in your abilities.

In addition, if the interviewer asks about you weaknesses, answer the question. We all have weaknesses, if you say "none" you have immediately lost trust from the interviewer. However, you do not have to confess all your shortcomings; choose one or two weaknesses you know how to overcome and explain how you overcame them.

This shows the employer that you are resourceful and a problem solver.

Lastly, know where your strengths and weaknesses are in your resume and job history, and be prepared to talk about them in the job interview. If your experience is limited, show the interviewer how you used your skill sets successfully in your previous jobs, and how they can be used in your new job. By preparing for the conversation ahead of time you will present yourself in a very positive light.

Make Eye Contact

Making positive eye contact is a key tip to acing an interview. Eye contact is so important because it is one of the strongest forms of nonverbal communication. A person's qualities and personality can be detected based on eye contact. Make direct eye contact to communicate confidence and high self-esteem, these are two key qualities employers look for in candidates.

You always hear, "keep good eye contact" but no one ever explains what they mean by "good" eye contact. You want to make sure that you are keeping eye contact on a pretty regular basis with the interviewer. However, you do not want to look like a psycho that is trying to stare them down! Keep your eye contact casual and natural, make sure you blink occasionally. Don't be too worried about breaking eye contact, as this is natural.

However, if you break eye contact go right back. We can only look at one eye at a time, make sure that you switch eyes every now and then; this is something we do without thinking but when we are nervous we tend to stare at only one eye. By maintaining good, natural eye contact you seem engaged with the interviewer and genuinely interested in what they are saying. If you still struggle with looking someone in the eye, look at the bridge of their nose between the eyes. To them it will look as though you are looking right at them but you are not.

Thus, it is very important that you make eye contact when you first meet the interviewer and shake hands. Moreover, during the interview, it is important to make eye contact, not only when you talk, but also as you listen. Practicing these two tips will greatly help your chances of success in a job interview.

Know Your Skills
You need to be very familiar with your resume and skill set before going on any interview. Remember, the interviewer is most likely meeting you for the first time and may not know much about you. Plus, the interviewer is probably meeting with several candidates for the same position, and you need to separate yourself from the crowd.

You must effectively communicate your skills and qualifications to the interviewer, and you can only do so if you are totally familiar with your resume and abilities.

For example, if they ask you what you learned from your last job, you should have a few answers to choose from. Moreover, every answer you give should be supported by concrete examples. Without concrete examples, the interviewer will have nothing to latch on to and might overlook what you have to say. However, if you attach a real-world event or accomplishment to your example, it is more likely to leave an impression on the interviewer; this is key to having a successful job interview.

Relax and Preserve your energy
When you get an interview it is very important to get as much sleep as you can the night before, you need to be able to walk into your interview exuding energy! Make sure to eat a good breakfast and if you are a coffee drinker don't forget to have some of that before you get there. Tip, after eating, and drinking coffee, make sure to pop in a breath mint a few minutes before the interview, even if you did brush your teeth.

Be watchful of tricky questions
Be watchful of tricky questions commonly asked during interviews such as questions on your weaknesses or why you left your previous employer. You don't have to make up stories but you can answer it in such a way that you are not putting down your previous employer. In the case of having to talk about your weakness, find a weakness that is not applicable to the type of job you are applying for or find a weakness that can be considered a strength.

Study the interviewer

Learning things about you interviewer can prevent you from making comments or references that can become awkward. You can also make references to things or ideas that strike a chord with your interviewer. You don't want to make it obvious that you researched your interviewer as you were searching for your online job. Research your interviewer on LinkedIn if they have a profile. Nevertheless, competition for jobs, especially through online job postings will be fierce. Any little advantage could be the difference between success and resuming your online job search.

Study the competition

Similar to the advantages of studying your potential employer, studying the potential employers industry can give you the leg up you need in your job search. Offering insights or quoting recent statistics about the industry can show a potential employer that you're serious about landing the job.

Be yourself

There must be things about you that the employer views as a positive for the job you're applying to or else you wouldn't be in the interview. Don't ruin that impression by trying to be someone you're not. Be yourself. Play up your strengths and be honest about your weaknesses, (but not too honest). Let the person they saw on the resume shine through.

Don't be the "stinky" person

Don't make the mistake of dousing yourself with cologne, or perfume, prior to the interview. If you are too "fragrant" the interviewer will be too taken aback by the smell and will not be focused on you, or the interview. Also, if you are a smoker, don't smoke prior to the interview. If the interviewer smells smoke on you it may affect you negatively. Your best bet is not to have any smell at all. Shower, put on clean clothes and wash your hands, that should be all that is needed. If you feel the need to wear perfume or cologne, remember the saying, "a little goes a long way."

Stay Positive

Forget about your hang-ups and past grievances with your previous job. Your bitterness will consume you, and reflect on your outlook and responses during the job interview. Embrace the fresh start, with a positive attitude. What has passed is in the past, do not let a bad experience, hinder your chances to start over. As unfortunate as it may be, life has to go on; by taking a step towards new a beginning with your job interview, you will be able to look beyond your misfortune. As long as you know that you can do anything and have the capacity and ability to achieve any goal, do not despair. With hope in your heart, face your job interview, free of doubts, and full of faith.

Be confident

You are standing at the entrance. You are nervous and don't know what to expect. You are thinking whether you will fumble and kick out halfway through? Fret not. Very likely it won't happen because you are well prepared for the interview. Half the battle is won. Just walk in with confidence and greet anyone you see with a big smile. Be nice and genuine but don't fake it. Nothing can be worse than a rubber stamped smile on your face. Some interviewers may purposely let you wait longer than expected to see how you will react in such a situation. Don't get impatient. Sometimes, they are really busy and can't leave their desk immediately.

Practice Answering Potential Interviewing Questions

Often, interviewers tend to ask many of the same types of questions. If you can practice and learn how to answer various types of questions, based on the job you're interviewing for, you will be able to sharpen your answers until they become second nature to you.

Post interview follow-up

After your interview, follow up with either a handwritten thank you note or an email immediately after the interview. Focus on the *value* that you will bring to the company. Don't just say "thank you," leave the door open for additional follow-up by saying that you will also follow up in a week to ten days. Don't worry about losing the job because of your follow-up. Employers expect well qualified and motivated candidates to follow up, be sure to do it in a respectful and professional manner.

Follow these tips and ace your job interviews with Hiring Managers.

CHAPTER 8
100 INTERVIEW QUESTIONS
AND ANSWERS YOU NEED TO
ACE TO GET HIRED

Interview preparation is the number #1 interview skill you need to stand out and get hired. These interview questions and answers will prepare you to ace an interview with any hiring manager or interviewer. A job interview is similar to learning how to play a musical instrument or sport. It takes practice to master the art of interviewing, and practice makes perfect. Most interviewers are not trying to torture you for sport. They ask tough questions to get right to the heart of specific issues and want to determine if you are a good fit for the company. Their motive is to quickly learn enough about you to make an informed decision about whether they should hire you or not. By the same token, if you know what the interviewer is looking for, you can craft your answers accordingly, and reduce your feelings of fear and anxiety at the same time.

The interviewing process is a type of sale. In this case, you are the product—and the salesperson. If you show up unprepared to talk about your unique features and benefits, you're not likely to motivate an interviewer to "buy."

The sad fact is that many job candidates are unprepared to talk about themselves. You may have emailed a stand out resume and cover letter. You may be wearing the perfect clothes on the day of the interview. But if you can't convince the interviewer—face to face—that you are the right person for the job, you aren't likely to make the sale (get hired).

Too many candidates hesitate after the first open-ended question, then stumble and stutter their way through a disjointed litany of resume "sound bites." Other interviewees recite canned replies that only highlight their memory skills.

Let's get right to the questions you might be asked and the best ways to answer these questions. Practice answering the following interview questions before all of your job interviews and stand out with hiring managers and interviewers.

Ace your interview questions and get hired.

Be prepared and confident!

Tell me about yourself.
This is usually the first question asked because it is a good icebreaker. You should not use this open-ended question to offer useless information about your hobbies and home life. Many people will make the mistake of saying, "I'm 32 years old, married, and a mother of three children ages 5, 7 and 9. My hobbies are knitting, cycling, reading and... blah blah blah." This is not a good answer.

Create a solid elevator pitch that will be memorable and make you stand out with any hiring manager or interviewer. A great elevator pitch for your job interviews will answer these three questions – "Describe who you are, what you do, and what you want" when the interviewer asks you the question, "Tell me about yourself."

A good answer to this question is about two minutes long and focuses on work-related skills and accomplishments. Tell the interviewer why you think your work-related skills and accomplishments would be an asset to the company. You could describe your education and work history (be brief) and then mention one or two personal character traits and tell the interviewer how those traits helped you accomplish a task at school or work. Do not describe yourself with tired old clichés such as "I am a team player," "I have excellent communication skills," unless you can prove it with an illustration. For example, one might say "I would describe myself as a self-starter. At Acme Corporation, there was a problem with... so I created a new inventory system (give details) that reduced expenses by 30 percent."

Someone with a new degree in an IT field might answer this question as follows: "I have enjoyed working with computers since I was eight years old and have always been adept as using them. Throughout junior high and high school, friends and relatives were always asking me for help with their computer problems, so no one was surprised when I chose to major in IT at college. I spent hundreds of hours learning about computers and how they work. A few years ago I became particularly interested in software development and began formulating ideas for a new software that would help consumers; I developed plans for a few computer applications on my own.

Where do you see yourself in five years?

Assume that you will be promoted two or three times in five years, so your answer should state that you see yourself working at whatever job is two or three levels above the job in which you are applying. Do not claim that you will be "running the company" in five years. You might want to add that you understand your promotions will be earned through hard work and that you do not assume you will be promoted just because you stayed with the company. Good answer: "I see myself as head of the Finance Department in five years. I've already proven that I have the ability to manage a large finance staff at Acme, and I expect that I will be promoted to a senior management position in the future provided I work hard at my job and earn the promotions, which is what I expect to do."

Are the company's goals and yours compatible? Are you looking for fast or steady growth in a position the interviewer knows is a virtual dead end? Are you requesting more money than he can ever pay? How have your goals and motivations changed as you have matured and gained work experience? If you've recently become a manager, how has that change affected your future career outlook? If you've realized you need to acquire or hone a particular skill, how and when are you planning to do so?

Naturally, you want a position of responsibility in your field. But you don't want to give the impression that you're a piranha waiting to feed on the guppies in your new department. So, start humbly by saying something like:

"Well, ultimately that will depend on my performance on the job, and on the growth and opportunities offered by my employer."

Then toot your horn a bit:
"I've already demonstrated leadership characteristics in all of the jobs I've held, so I'm very confident that I will take on progressively greater management responsibilities in the future. That suits me fine. I enjoy building a team, developing its goals, and then working to accomplish them. It's very rewarding."

In other words, you want "more"—more responsibility, more people reporting to you, more turf, and more money. A general answer (as above) is okay, but don't be surprised when an interviewer asks the obvious follow-up questions (using the answer to the above question as a guide): "Tell me about the last team you led a project;" "Tell me about the last project your team undertook;" "What was the most satisfying position you've held, and why?" "If I told you our growth was phenomenal and you could go as far as your abilities would take you, where would that be, and how quickly?"

Do not respond with an answer that reveals unrealistic expectations. A savvy candidate should have some idea of the time it takes to climb the career ladder in a particular industry or even in a company. Someone hoping to go from receptionist to CEO in two years will, of course, scare off most interviewers, but any expectations that are far too ambitious could give them pause. If a law school grad, for example, seeks to make partner in four years—when the average for all firms is seven and, for this one, 10—this will make even novice interviewers question the extent and effectiveness of your pre-interview research.

There's nothing wrong with being ambitious and confident beyond all bounds, but a savvy interviewee should temper such boundless expectations during the interview, knowing full well that some candidates do "break the rules" successfully, most interviewers get a little nervous about people with completely unbridled ambition!

Are you willing to relocate?

If relocating were not an issue, the interviewer would not be asking the question. Therefore, the only acceptable answer is "Yes." If you answer in the negative, you will not get the job. If you really do not want to relocate, then perhaps you should not accept the job if it is subsequently offered to you. If you are not sure, then ask questions about relocation, such as when it will likely occur, where you will be required to relocate, and will it involve a promotion.

Are you willing to travel?

If traveling were not part of the job, the interviewer would not be asking this question. Therefore, the only acceptable answer is "yes." If you are willing to travel, answer "yes" and give some illustrations of work travel you have done. However, if you do not want to travel, you should find out more about this aspect of the job before accepting the position, such as how much travel will be involved, where will you be traveling to and for how long.

Are you willing to work overtime?

If this wasn't an aspect of the job, the interviewer wouldn't be asking this question. Therefore, the only acceptable answer is "yes" if you want to be considered for the job. If your past jobs involved overtime, now would be the time to tell this to the interviewer.

What book are you currently reading? What was the last book you read? What were the last three books you read?

The only correct answer is to offer the title of a non-fiction book, preferably one that is on a subject related to your career or business in general. For example, if you are a sales person, tell the reader you're currently in the middle of, "Selling for Dummies." Alternatively, if that seems too much of a cliché, offer the title of a book on improving your time management, personality, efficiency, etc. Of course, we are not suggesting that you lie and claim to be reading a book that you aren't really reading. As part of your job search, you will have to start reading one or two acceptable books so that you can intelligently discuss them if the subject is brought up during an interview. The interviewer might ask you how the book is helping you (what you have learned from it), so have an answer ready. Some interviewers will try to determine if you regularly read by asking you for titles of three to five books you've read this year, so be ready.

What is the last movie you saw?

Replying that you "don't have time to watch movies as you are completely devoted to your job" is not a good answer and will not win you any points, even if the interviewer is naive enough to believe you. Interviewers are looking for well-rounded people who enjoy healthy activities, such as relaxation and entertainment, and will expect you to state the name of a movie. The movie title that you give in response to this question should always be one that is popular with the general public, but not controversial, meaning that it doesn't have any negative or zealous political or religious overtones. Also, don't reveal the fact that you spend way too much time watching movies by stating you have seen a particular movie fifteen times or that you spend too much time watching movies. For example, don't tell the interviewer that you are obsessed with Star Trek movies and regularly attend Star Trek conventions dressed up as Mr. Spock. A well-known uncontroversial movie, popular with the general public, and one that the interviewer is likely to have seen, is always a good choice.

What are your hobbies and interests outside of work?

The interviewer is trying to find out (1) more about who you are and (2) if you maintain an interest in a particular subject for a long period. You should not indicate that you change hobbies frequently or have a problem maintaining an interest in one subject over a long period. A good answer might be, "I have been interested in ge-nealogy for the past five years. I am currently the President of the Adams County Genealogical Society and we meet once a month to exchange research tips. It's very interesting, but I don't have much time with my busy schedule to do much research now, but I plan to spend more time doing research after I retire." Answers that reveal participation in sports are also good: "For the past five years I have been an avid racquetball player. I've competed in a dozen or so competitions and I've won a few." Of course, you do not want to reveal any hobby or activity that most people would consider strange, such as "I collect the autographs of convicted serial killers."

What do you like to watch on television?

In answering this question, one should not appear too silly or too arrogant. Therefore, avoid revealing the fact that you have seen every episode of the Brady Bunch two hundred times or that you race home from work everyday to hear the Gilligan's Island theme song. Don't swing to the opposite extreme and claim that you never watch television or only watch PBS and C-SPAN because they will know you're lying or think you are weird or boring. The best answer reveals that you do watch television, but you watch respectable, very popular programs such as "Law and Order" or "CSI." Never admit to being a couch potato who sits in front of the TV five hours everyday.

Good answer 1: "I don't watch that much television. I try to catch the news everyday, I like to watch political programs on Sunday mornings, and football in the fall. "60 Minutes" is probably my favorite program. My family and I usually find a movie to watch on Saturday and Sunday nights. Sometimes we rent a few movies on weekends, but I don't really have any favorite programs I watch consistently every week."

Good answer 2: "I enjoy watching "Friends" just like millions of other Americans. I get together with six or so friends at a pizza place on Thursday nights and we watch it together. I rent a few movies on most weekends, and I do try to catch the news every morning when I'm getting ready for work. I don't have that much time for television because I work and go to school full time. And the last thing I want to do after sitting all day in class and at work is to come home and sit in front of the television. In my free time, I usually go to the gym, walk my dog and spend time with my friends and family rather than watch television."

What jobs did you have as a teenager?

Answer this question honestly. Either you had jobs or you didn't. Household chores, mowing lawns, shoveling snow, and lemonade stands all count as jobs.

Good answer 1: "I worked part-time at both Burger King and McDonalds between the ages of 16 and 20 in order to earn money to buy my first car and help my parents pay for my college education. I was able to handle both work and school without my grades suffering. And when I was younger, around 13 to 16 years old, I babysat for families in the neighborhood on weekends."

Good answer 2: "I didn't have any jobs as a child other than chores I was expected to do around the house such as helping my parents with housekeeping, mowing the lawn, shoveling snow, and babysitting my younger sister and brother. My parents placed tremendous emphasis on academics and extracurricular activities, and would not allow me to work."

Who are your references?

It is a good idea to print the names and contact information of your references on a sheet of paper and present it to the interviewer when the topic comes up. Ideally, one should provide the names of former supervisors or co-workers as references since these are the people prospective employers most want to speak with about your work performance. Giving the names of others as references -- such as friends, family members, etc. -- might be an indication that you do not want the interviewer to contact your supervisor. If you do not have any work history, use teachers, professors, or business people you or your family knows as references.

A good answer to this question: "I prepared a list of references for you. I have included the names of my two previous supervisors at Acme, Jack Wilson and Norma Smith who can speak about my work performance and accomplishments."

If you do not have any work references, a good answer might be, "I asked two of my engineering professors to be references for me and they agreed to do so. I printed their names, phone numbers and contact information for you. They can attest to the work I completed as an intern over the past two years. I also listed Mrs. Sally Wilson, who is a prominent attorney and a friend of the family. She has known me since I was a child and can attest to my character."

Do you mind if I contact your references?

Say, yes you can contact my former employers or the references you provide the interviewer. You should always keep your job search confidential. You don't ever want your current boss to know you're searching for a new job. Tell the interviewer: "You may contact Mr. Jack Smith, my former supervisor at Acme. He supervised me for four years and agreed to be a reference for me."

Will you take a Lie-Detector Test?

The interviewer is asking this question (1) because it is a requirement to get the job, or (2) to find out if you are afraid of the prospect of taking such a test. Therefore, the only correct answer to this question is "Yes, I am willing to take a lie detector test." You don't need to say anything else.

How do you feel about air travel?

Obviously, the interviewer wouldn't be asking this question if traveling by air wasn't an important component of the job, so the only correct way to answer this question is "No, I have no problem with air travel." You might want to expand your answer by telling the interviewer that you traveled a lot in a previous job. If you tell the interviewer you are afraid of flying or cannot do so for some other reason, such as a medical condition, you might not get the job offer.

Have you ever owned your own business?

The best answer to this question is "yes" since it shows initiative and that you have had some experience with marketing services or products. Good answer: "Yes, I ran my own business while in high school. I went door-to-door asking people if they needed their lawns mowed. I earned a substantial amount of money in a few months, enough to pay for a car and my first year of college." If you have never owned your own business just say no.

Are you in good health?

The interviewer is asking this question because providing health insurance to employees costs employers a small fortune. Consequently, many employers prefer to hire those who try to maintain their health to keep the number of claims down and insurance rates as low as possible. Keep in mind that employers can find out your medical history and many of them make the job offer contingent upon your passing a physical examination, therefore, it wouldn't be a good idea to blatantly lie about your medical history. That doesn't mean you should offer information you don't have to, such as "I smoked cigarettes for thirty years, but gave them up last year" or "I've had two heart attacks and a stroke". If your health is generally good, then answer this question briefly: "Yes, I'm in good health" or "I have no health problems that would prevent me from doing this job" and don't elaborate any further.

What do you do to maintain your health?

Obviously, if you're in good shape, answering this question is easy: "I jog two or three nights a week and lift weights at the Acme Gym three times a week. I try to eat a balanced diet; I eat lots of salads and try to maintain my weight."

If you're overweight or obese (as are 65% of adult Americans) answering this question isn't going to be easy. Here is a sample answer: "I walk my dogs for 45 minutes every night. I recently started the Atkins diet program and have lost seven pounds. It's a diet I can live with, so I know this time I'll be able to lose weight and start taking better care of my health."

Do you have any physical problems that would limit your ability to perform this job?

Employers have to be very careful about asking this question as too much prying can violate your civil rights. Therefore, they won't ask too many questions and you don't need to offer them very much information. The best way to answer this question is to keep it short and simple: "No, I don't have any physical problems that would affect my ability to perform this job."

Are you a member of any organizations?

The interviewer is interested in work-related memberships, not personal ones. The fact that you are a member of the American Business Association is more important than your participation in your local PTA (which reveals the fact that you have children). It is also a good idea not to reveal religious and political affiliations, such as memberships in the Democratic Party, Republican Party, or any political or ethnic and cultural affiliations.

How do you balance career and family?

On the surface this questions appears to be illegal, but it isn't because of the way it's worded. The interviewer is hoping you will reveal information about things he isn't allowed to ask, such as if you are married, single, divorced, have children, or are straight or gay. If you don't want to reveal information about your personal life, offer the interviewer a vague simple answer such as: "I haven't had a problem balancing my work and private life; one has never interfered with the other. I am capable of getting the work I need to get done without it interfering with my personal life."

On the other hand, you might want to reveal a great deal of information if you think it will help you get the job offer: "I can easily balance my career and family life as my children are now in college and my wife is starting a new career as a real estate agent. We both work hard and have flexible schedules to work when we need to, but we still have a good personal life, spending time with friends and family every week."

What are your greatest strengths?

Provide one or two strengths that are work-related and give the interviewer an example that proves you possess that strength. Sample answer: "I have the ability to train and motivate people. For example, at Acme Corporation, employee turnover was sixty percent. In an effort to find out why, I interviewed more than 200 employees. I discovered a major reason for the high turnover was lack of proper training and low morale. To solve the problem, I developed a training program that helped motivate workers to perform their jobs better and work smarter. Each training session lasted only two days, but the results were impressive -- productivity improved 30 percent and employee turnover was reduced by more than half."

What are your greatest weaknesses?

Don't answer this question by claiming that you have no weaknesses. Confess a real weakness that you have, but choose one that isn't particularly relevant to the job you're seeking. Do not answer with phony weaknesses such as "I'm a workaholic at my job." Just state the weakness, tell the interviewer how it has harmed you in your work life, and what steps you have taken to improve it. A good step one can take to improve a weakness is to read self-help books on the subject. You might offer the title of a book you've read that helped you improve your weakness.

Sample answer 1: "A major weakness I had in the past was delegating work to others and trusting them to do it correctly. In my early career, this caused some problems for me in that my subordinates were unhappy because they felt I lacked confidence in them. I would try to do the work myself or look over their shoulders while they were doing the work. This problem was brought to my attention by my supervisor in a performance review. I agreed with her on this point and admitted I needed to change so I read a few self-help books that helped me change my thinking and let go of the idea that I needed to micromanage my work environment in order to get the job done. Now, I have no problem delegating work to subordinates."

Sample answer 2: "I'm shy until I get to know a person. Being shy has cost me a great deal in my career as it has prevented me from getting promotions and jobs I've wanted. A few years ago, I realized I would have to change or I wasn't going to achieve my career goals. I read several self-help books on the subject, "Getting Over Your Shyness" was one, and I summoned up the courage to take a speech class at night. The teacher was excellent and was able to convince me how shyness is just an irrational fear. Although I'll always be shy, I'm not nearly as shy as I used to be and I've greatly improved my ability to communicate with others by taking several more speech classes. Now, I can get up in front of a large group of people and give a lengthy presentation without a problem."

Bad answer: "I have a major weakness for chocolate." Although this is a weakness, to offer this as an answer is to sidestep the question and will turn off the interviewer.

Do you work best alone or as part of a team?

If the position you're applying for requires you to spend lots of time alone, then of course, you should state that you like to work alone and vice versa. Never sound too extreme one way or the other. Don't say that you hate people and would "die if you had to work with others" and don't state that you "will go crazy if you're left alone for five minutes." A healthy balance between the two is always the best choice. If you have previous experience illustrating the fact that you can work alone or with others, then offer it. For example, you might state that in your previous job you spent a significant amount of time alone while traveling, or that you have learned how to get along well with people in the workplace by working on numerous team projects.

Do you consider yourself to be organized? Do you manage your time well?

The interviewer wants to hear about your work skills concerning time and task management, not that you have neatly separated the paperclips in your desk drawer into different trays based on size. A model answer might be "I manage my time very well. I routinely complete tasks ahead of schedule. For example,.. (offer the interviewer proof of your organizational skills by telling him about a major project that you organized and completed on time, or mention that you consistently received an outstanding score on previous performance reviews regarding time management). Do not reveal to the interviewer that you are habitually late or that you complete tasks at the very last minute.

Do you consider yourself to be a risk-taker?

How you answer this question depends on the type of company it is. If it is a start-up company or within a highly-competitive industry, then they are probably looking for those more willing to take risks. If you believe the company is this type, then offer an example of a risk you've taken in business. If the company is a well-established industry leader, risk takers are not as highly valued. Of course, no company is looking for employees who are foolish in their risk-taking behavior, so a good rule of thumb is to place yourself somewhere in the middle -- you are neither too foolish nor overly cautious.

Are you a self-starter?

The correct answer to this question is always "yes," and the ideal answer includes an example of how you are able to work with minimal supervision, keep your skills current without being told, or a time when you took it upon yourself to be more efficient, accurate or productive.

Example 1: "Yes, I am definitely a self-starter. When I worked at Acme Corporation, I was positive that the firm would be adopting a new operating system within a year, so I started taking classes at the local university at night in order to prepare myself. I was the only one in the office that knew how to operate the equipment when it was installed, so I was appointed trainer and subsequently trained 200 co-workers. I received recognition for my work on that project."

Example 2: "Yes, I am a self-starter. I am always thinking of ways I can improve office efficiency and help the company be more profitable. For example, a few years ago I noticed that the sales reps were having a difficult time finding client files. The sales reps would put client's on hold and spend as much as five minutes looking for a file. I developed a file management system that enabled the sales reps to locate client files on their desktops in less than 15 seconds. This has made the office much more efficient and, of course, made both the sales reps and our clients much happier."

How do you react to criticism from supervisors that you consider unjust?

The only correct way to answer this question is to present yourself as a person who can handle criticism without becoming angry, defensive, vengeful or arrogant, yet, not let others intimidate or blame you when you don't deserve it. Example: "There was a time when I was deeply hurt when a supervisor pointed out a mistake I made or an area in which I needed to improve and felt somewhat defensive. However, through the years, I have learned that no one is perfect; everyone makes mistakes and needs to improve in certain areas, so I shouldn't take criticism so personally. Therefore, I have learned to take it on the chin without becoming defensive or feeling hurt. I just take a few days to think about what was said and if I feel the criticism is warranted, I take steps to improve my performance. If I feel the criticism was unjustified, I will sit down with my supervisor and calmly discuss the reasons why I feel the criticism was unjustified."

How well do you handle change?

The only acceptable answer is one stating you handle change very well. Don't just make this claim; offer an example of how well you coped with a major change that took place in your work environment. A common shakeup occurs when your employer brings in new automation or changes its culture. In any event, tell the interviewer what you did to cope or adapt to a change that occurred with a previous employer -- and this should be a major change, not a minor one.

Are you opposed to doing a lot of routine work?

Don't answer with, "Oh yes, I will enjoy filing eight hours a day, 40 hours a week, 50 weeks a year!" Instead, try to assure the interviewer you aren't going to go mad doing your boring job. For example, "I know this position requires a lot of routine work, but I don't expect to start at the top. I'm willing to start at the bottom and prove myself. Eventually, I will be assigned tasks that require more brain power."

How do you resolve disputes with co-workers and handle conflicts?

Don't claim that you have never had a dispute with a co-worker. The interviewer will know you are fibbing, since getting along with all co-workers is unusual -- there's always at least one difficult person that can be a challenge to work with. The best answer to this question tells the interviewer about a dispute you had with a co-worker and how you resolved it so that the outcome was positive. Your answer should tell the interviewer how you resolved it on your own, and hopefully, that you and this other person are now friends, or at least are able to work together productively. Also, concentrate on offering an example of how you resolved a work-related conflict rather than disclosing a personal feud over some petty subject. For example, telling the interviewer about your problems getting a co-worker to take your suggestions on a specific project seriously is a much better topic than telling the interviewer about your feud with another co-worker over a parking space. In addition, don't tell the interviewer that you resolved a dispute by tattling to the boss or trying to get the other person fired. Employers are sick of dealing with employee conflicts and they want a mature person who can resolve conflicts on her own without tattling or complaining to the boss.

What reference books do you use at work?

One should not answer this question, "I don't have any reference books." A good, safe answer is to state that you use a dictionary on a regular basis and one or two other books that are relevant to your field. For example, if you are a sales person you might respond, "I keep a dictionary handy and the book that helped me succeed in sales, "How to Win Friends and Influence People." If your work involves accounting, then mention a few accounting reference books; if your work involves computer programming, then mention a few relevant computer programming books, and so on.

Have you ever held a position that wasn't right for you?

One can answer this question either yes or no, but answering "no" would be better. If you answer yes, then you need to explain the mistake you made in exercising good judgment, and a good reason is always the lure of more money. For example, one might answer: "A good friend of mine convinced me that I could make six figures quite easily selling real estate, so I gave up my job as an office manager and jumped right in. I soon realized I wasn't cut out for that world because there were too many players and I didn't have the necessary connections. Had I known that fewer than 10% of real estate agents manage to make a decent living, I never would have entered the field. I stayed in real estate for a year before I realized I was not going to make a six figure income, so I quit and found another position as an office manager, which is work that I am good at and like doing."

What is your most significant career accomplishment?

Just answer this question honestly. You don't have to be Albert Einstein and say "I discovered the theory of relativity." A good answer: "I think my most significant career accomplishment is rising from a receptionist to a district manager at Acme in just five years. I started there with no education and no training, and I worked hard all day and went to school at night until I earned a master's degree in management." Another good answer: "I think my most significant career accomplishment was winning the XYZ account at Acme, which brought my employer $30 million in sales and helped establish the company as an international player. It wasn't easy winning that account because we were competing with a dozen or so competitors who could offer a more high-tech product at a lower price, but I was able to put together a package that convinced management at XYZ that our company was better for them in the long-term."

Are you comfortable working for a large company?

The interviewer might be asking this question because your employment history shows you've always worked for smaller companies. Always answer this question in the positive, "Yes, I would be very comfortable working for a large company. I believe that working for a large company would not only provide more opportunities for advancement and growth, but would also expose me to more areas in my field."

Are you comfortable working for a small company?

The interviewer might be asking this question because your employment history shows you've always worked for larger companies and doubts you will be able to fit into a new environment. Always answer this question in the positive, "Yes, after working for a large corporation the past five years, I look forward to working for a small company where employees work more closely with one another and there is more of an informal team effort rather than the cold, impersonal corporate atmosphere. I did work for smaller companies at the start of my career and have always missed that atmosphere and look forward to it again."

How long do you think you will work for us?

When answering this question, keep in mind that it costs employers a small fortune to hire you. They spend thousands of dollars recruiting and training you; therefore, they don't want you to stay for just a few months or years and then quit. However, don't assume the interviewer wants your answer to be "I will be your most devoted employee until I retire forty years from now," particularly if your resume indicates you generally stay with one employer for five years (as most Americans do) before moving on.

Many HR experts recommend that you answer this question: "I will stay as long as I continue to grow and make a positive contribution to the company" but this answer has become somewhat of a cliché. Formulate your answer based on your age, your field, and your work history.

Good answer 1: "If I am offered this position, I plan to stay with this company until I retire about ten years from now. At this time in my life, I've begun to plan for my eventual retirement. This position offers an excellent retirement package and seems to come with many opportunities for growth, and I think I would have exciting and challenging work to perform for the remainder of my career."

Good answer 2: "If I am offered this position, I plan to stay with this company for a long time since there are many opportunities for growth and the position is one that would enable me to do quite a bit of software development work, which is my passion. This position gives me the opportunity to learn many different facets of the software development process and it will take me awhile to achieve everything I want to achieve at this job."

Do you anticipate problems or just react to them?

The correct answer to this question is that you try to anticipate problems rather than react to them. Give a brief outline of a time when you caught a problem and resolved it before it damaged the company. Good answer: "I always try to anticipate problems and resolve them before they occur. For example, at Acme I knew that there were bugs in the system that would eventually surface. I was able to catch numerous problems with the network before they occurred by running tests on the system to locate these bugs. I located and fixed several errors in the network design that prevented a significant amount of system downtime. By anticipating this problem and fixing it, I was able to reduce network downtime to almost zero."

How do you handle (resolve) problems with co-workers?

Employers want employees who can resolve problems with co-workers on their own without getting a supervisor involved and who can work well with co-workers without disrupting the work environment. Therefore, a good answer to this question tells the interviewer that you have had conflicts with co-workers (because everyone has) but you resolved them on your own. Good answer: "I haven't had that many conflicts with co-workers, but there was one particular co-worker who would make sarcastic, biting remarks to me while we worked. I think she was jealous because I was much younger than she was and I was the only other female in the sales department. Finally, one day I sat down with her and asked her why she was so sarcastic to me. She denied it; however, the comments stopped after we talked, and eventually, we became friends."

Tell me what you do on a typical day at work.

The interviewer is trying to discover (1) if you exaggerated the job duties listed on your resume and/or (2) if you have the necessary experience to perform the job for them. Consequently, your answer should emphasize duties one would perform in the job you're trying to get. If you can, reread the job description and emphasize the job duties listed there. Good answer: "On a typical day, I arrive at work around 7:30 and look over various departmental reports in order to prepare myself for the morning meeting with the sales staff. From 8:30 to 10:00, I meet with a 30 member sales staff. We have training sessions, motivational sessions, we discuss problems and try to solve them. From 10:00 to noon, I'm on the phone, chatting with various, clients, department heads, and government agencies. In the afternoon, I'm either out in the field, visiting various stores in the area or attending meetings with clients."

Why do you want to leave your present employer?

You could state that you want a more challenging position, higher salary, or more responsibility. Don't mention personal conflicts with your present boss or bad-mouth your current employer or co-workers as this will harm your chances of being offered the job. Keep in mind that interviewers love people who are looking for more challenging positions or responsibility because it shows drive, ambition and motivation.

What did your last supervisor criticize most about your performance?

A good way to answer this question is to offer a criticism you received that is not very important or not directly related to the position for which you are applying. For example, telling the interviewer that you were constantly criticized for coming to work an hour late is not a good idea. However, revealing a minor criticism and telling the interviewer what steps you took to improve yourself is a good way to answer this question. In fact, if you can state that you have already solved the problem and received a higher mark on a subsequent performance review, then say so.

Have you ever been fired or asked to resign?

Honesty is always the best policy when answering this question. Always tell the truth when answering this question, keep in mind that the interviewer knows that almost everyone has been fired at least once and it is usually due to a personality conflict with the boss or coworkers. So, if you have been fired then admit it, but do so without attacking your former boss or employer, and without sounding defensive or bitter. Do not mention that you have been fired many times unless asked specifically, "How many times have you been fired?" Tell the interviewer what you learned from being fired. If you have been fired many times, mention what steps you have taken to improve yourself (i.e., I have read self-help books about... getting along with others... improving my time management... improving knowledge, work habits, etc.). Also, point out any past jobs you held when you got along well with your boss and coworkers or received good performance reviews or a promotion.

How long have you been searching for a job? Why haven't you received a job offer? Why have you been unemployed for so long?

It is always best to answer this question with "I just started looking" but this is not always possible, particularly if your resume indicates you've been unemployed for the last six months. If you can't hide the fact that your job search has been taking awhile, then state that you're being selective about whom you will work for. Of course, stating this might prompt the interviewer to ask, "What offers have you turned down?". Tell the interviewer I would like to keep the job offers confidential.

What previously held job do you consider to be your favorite and why?

This is actually a trick question asked to determine if you enjoy the type of work the position you're applying for involves. Therefore, the answer to this question should be a job that requires the same or similar work that you will be required to perform in the new job. If you do not have a previous job wherein you performed similar tasks, then offer an answer that does not suggest you are ill-suited for the position. For example, if you are applying for a high-stress, demanding job in a chaotic environment, don't tell the interviewer you loved your position with Acme because of the mellow, low stress "work at your own pace" atmosphere.

Would you choose the same career if you could start over again?

How you answer this question depends on whether or not you are trying to win a job related to your career history or are trying to enter a new field. No matter how much you despise the career you originally chose, do not admit this fact to the interviewer because it tells him you consider your work to be a drudge. If you are trying to enter a new field, of course, tell the interviewer that you would choose the field you're now trying to enter if you had it to do all over again -- that's why you're trying to enter it now.

Why have you stayed with the same employer for so long?

Just as moving from job to job too frequently can harm you, so can staying with the same employer for too long -- particularly if you've never been promoted and your resume indicates you haven't been intellectually challenged in years. Your answer should state something about your having worked successfully with many people both inside and outside of the organization, including different bosses and co-workers, as well as interacting regularly with various types of organizations and customers.

Why have you changed jobs so frequently?

Your reasons for job-hopping should be based on your past employers' failure to challenge you, failure to give you enough opportunity for advancement, because you needed more money, or for family reasons, and never on the basis that your past employers were incompetent, dumb, or unfair. Do not indicate in any way that you are hard to get along with or get bored and leave at the drop of a hat. Make sure you point out any jobs you held for a long period of time. Mention that your current goal is long-term employment and back that up with any proof you have to want job stability such as a new baby, new marriage, new home, etc. If the job you're applying for offers you the challenges and environment you were always looking for, make sure you point out this fact.

Good answer 1: "Well, at ABC Corporation, I was hired as an entry level salesman with the promise of rapid promotion to management within one year. After a year and a half, I realized that I wasn't going to be promoted as promised and took a position elsewhere because I could not support my family without the commissions that were promised. At Acme, I was told that the job was very challenging and exciting with significant opportunities for advancement within one year, but this did not materialize. The job was very unchallenging and the company seemed to be failing. I felt like I was capable of doing much more than sitting around with little to do, so I left. I admit that my resume shows some job hopping of late, but this is why I am so interested in the position with your company. I feel certain that this position offers challenging and interesting work, as well as opportunities for advancement for those willing to work hard. Your company is profitable and stable and has a good reputation in the industry. I know this will be a position I will stay with for a long time."

Good answer 2: "I do not believe that my work history is an accurate reflection of who I am. I am actually a stable person who would enjoy working for the same employer for a long period. Note that on my resume, it indicates that I worked for XYZ Company for five years in the early 1990s. I admit that my resume indicates some job hopping in the late 1990s, but this was because I was caring for my elderly, sick mother between 1995 and 2001. Caring for her required being available nights and on weekends, so I was not able to work overtime as the job at Acme required. I had to resign after working there for only a year. At XYZ Industries, I had to resign after only one year because they insisted on transferring me to the west coast. I simply could not move away from my mother who was too elderly and ill to make such a move. My mother passed away in 2001, I got married a year later and had a child. Now, I have a wife and child to support and a mortgage to pay. I am eager to settle down and work for a company like yours for a long period of time."

Who was your favorite boss and why? Who was your least favorite boss and why?

These are two of the most difficult interview questions to answer unless you understand what the interviewer wants to hear, and if you think about it you can answer both questions with the same answer. Employers are looking for employees who are interested in contributing to the company and improving their job skills. So, instead of insulting or demeaning your past bosses by telling the interviewer that they were always "hogging all the credit" or were "totally incompetent," state that you wished they had offered you more feedback about your job performance, provided you with more job training, or challenged you more by providing you with more opportunities to show what you can do, etc. You can answer the question, "Who was your favorite boss and why?" using the same answer: "John Doe was my favorite boss because he offered me lots of feedback about my job performance, taught me almost everything I know about marketing, and gave me plenty of opportunities to prove myself by giving me very challenging projects to complete." Never put down past employers or blame them for anything in a demeaning or insulting way, since it makes you come across as petty.

What could you have done to improve your relationship with your least favorite boss?

Again, refrain from stating negativities about your former boss. Put a positive spin on your answer by telling the interviewer that, if you had it to do all over again, you would have requested more feedback from your boss regarding your performance and requested to be assigned more projects, etc.

What Is The Most Foolish Thing You've Ever Done?

Do not answer this question by claiming that you have never done anything foolish, because everyone has done something foolish. The ideal answer would be to admit a foolish thing you did in your personal life a long time ago (perhaps as a teenager) rather than admit a foolish mistake done in your recent professional life. For example, one might answer, "When I was 14 years old, I decided to steal my father's car keys and go for a joy ride. Unfortunately, my driving skills weren't as good as I thought they were and I crashed into a telephone pole less than a mile from home. I was so afraid of my father's reaction, that I left the car there and ran to a friend's house. I did some other silly things as a kid, but fortunately, I've never done anything I consider to be foolish as an adult or at work. Of course, I have made some mistakes at work, but I've learned from them and didn't consider them to be foolish."

Have any of your past employers refused to give you a reference?

Of course, the best answer to this question is "no", but if you have to answer "yes," explain why in a professional manner. In other words, don't complain bitterly about the employer who refused to give you a reference. Sample answer: "Yes, John Wilson at Acme refuses to give me a reference because he is unhappy that I resigned from the company. This is unfortunate because John and I liked each other and we worked well together. I received excellent performance reviews and two raises based on performance while at Acme; his refusal to give me a reference is not based on poor performance. As I said, he is angry at me for resigning because he considers my doing so to be disloyal to the company." Sample answer 1: "Yes, Acme Corporation refuses to give me a reference; however, this is not based on performance. Acme has been sued many times by former employees so they have adopted the policy of confirming only job title, work dates and salary through Human Resources. If you contact Mr. Wilson at Acme, he will likely not respond or will refer you to Human Resources. This is not based on my performance, but rather, on company policy."

Why are there gaps in your employment history?

Answer this question by explaining each recent gap in your work history that is longer than six months. Put a positive spin on your answer; good reasons to explain away employment gaps are that you took some time off to raise your children or to go back to school and get your degree or obtain necessary training to get a better job. Although not ideal, acceptable reasons to explain employment gaps are that you took a year off to travel or that the economy has been very bad and you simply couldn't find work in a year and a half. Don't say it was because "no one would hire me" or "I kept getting fired" without putting a positive spin on your answer. Mention that your current goal is long-term employment and back that up with any proof you have to want job stability such as a new baby, new marriage, new home, etc. If the job you're applying for offers you the challenges and environment you were always looking for, you should point out this fact.

Good answer 1: "The reason there is a two year gap in my employment history is because I could afford to be very choosy as I had a substantial amount of money in savings, which allowed me to spend almost two years looking for the right position. I resigned from Acme Corporation because the work was very unchallenging and I wanted to make sure I found a new position that offered me the type of challenging, interesting work and advancement for opportunities I was searching for. So, I interviewed for many positions and was offered quite a few of them, but I turned them down because they were not right for me."

Good answer 2: "When I was younger, I did some foolish things, one of which was not having any idea of what I wanted to do with my life, so I was generally unfocused and ended up quitting several good jobs so I could attend school full-time and get the necessary training to enter a new field. The two-year employment gap between my job at Acme and XYZ Industries occurred because I was attending school full-time while my wife supported us financially. The most recent employment gap occurred because I again decided to go back to school and earn a degree so I could qualify for better jobs."

Would your present employer be surprised to know you're job hunting?

Never answer this question with negative information such as "My current boss wouldn't be surprised in the least to hear I'm leaving since he's been trying to shove me out the door for years!" Always tell the interviewer that you are happy with your current employer and job, but are simply looking to stretch your wings out and take on a job with more challenge, and yes, more salary and opportunities for advancement.

How would your co-workers describe you?

Obviously, you don't want to say your co-workers would describe you as a troubled loner. The only correct answer to this question is to say that they would describe you as a pleasant person who works well with others. Put forth other positive traits about yourself as well: hard-working, efficient, dependable, easy going, funny, witty, etc.

Good answer: "My coworkers would describe me as a pleasant, nice person who is very dependable and hard-working. I tend to be shy at first, but after people get to know me, I come out of my shell and am very fun to be around."

What would you do if a supervisor asked you to do something the wrong way?

The interviewer is testing how insubordinate you might be. Never answer this question by claiming you would refuse to do something the way the supervisor told you to do it unless you are required by your company or by law to follow certain procedures. Instead, tell the interviewer you would tell the supervisor you think it should be done another way, but if the supervisor insisted you do it his way, you would do so.

Good answer: "If I was aware that there was a more efficient or better way to perform a task, I would tactfully point this out to the supervisor. However, if she still wanted me to do it her way, I would do so."

What types of people do you have trouble getting along with?

You don't want to answer this question with "Hard-working people who make lazy people like me look bad." You want to be the hard-working, nice person who doesn't like lazy or difficult people. However, be careful, the position you're interviewing for might come with an unpleasant, difficult supervisor and the interviewer is asking you this question for that reason.

Good answer 1: "I don't get along well with people who don't hold up their end of the job, who are constantly coming in late or calling in sick. They don't really respect their co-workers and bring the whole organization down."

Good answer 2: "I don't get along well with people who are opinionated and close-minded. They always seem to be complaining about one thing or another and they're unpleasant to be around."

Why should we hire you?

Take several minutes to answer this question, incorporating your personality traits, strengths, and experience into the job you're applying for. A good answer is to focus on how you can benefit the company. You can best do this by matching your skills and qualifications to those needed for the job and be ready with examples of how your skills, talents, and so on, mesh with the needs of that particular company.

Sample answer 1: "You should hire me because I have considerable experience and success in marketing software products to small companies. I know that your organization has not done well serving the small business sector and would like to greatly expand sales in this segment. At Acme, I was able to increase small business accounts 60 percent in just two years. At XYZ Corporation, I single-handedly brought in 260 new small business accounts in just three years, which was a company record. Currently, your company has a very high turnover rate among sales recruits, approximately 60 percent. I succeeded in reducing employee turnover by more than 30% at both Acme and XYZ. I also had great success in leading and motivating new sales recruits. A large percentage of those I have trained have gone on to be stellar performers. This is why you should hire me. I can make a positive impact on sales and help reduce labor costs, making this company more competitive and profitable."

Sample answer 2: "I believe I am the best person for this position because you need an office manager who can work effectively with diverse employees in a fast-paced environment. I have more than a decade of experience supervising clerical workers from diverse cultures, helping them to become more productive and efficient. I have reduced employee turnover by more than 20% in the past three years, which saved my employer more than $1 million in related hiring and training costs each of those three years. I also eliminated the need for 10% of the office staff by automating several processes, saving my employer a small fortune in labor costs. I am confident that I can resolve your current labor problems, reduce your labor costs significantly while improving worker morale and productivity."

What do you know about our company?

Those who answer this question with, "Not much," will probably not be offered the job. You should always research a company before the interview. Learn about their products/services, size, plans, current events, etc. If you cannot find information about a particular company, call their offices and ask the receptionist to send you information about the company in the form of a brochure. You should also research the industry in which the company operates so you are up on what's happening. Do a Google search to obtain as much information as you can about the company with which you will be interviewing. Also visit sites such as Glassdoor to learn more about companies and what current and former employees are saying.

Why do you want this position?

Your answer should offer what you think are the most interesting aspects of the position. More responsibility and opportunity, including a higher salary, are acceptable answers, but state them in a way that isn't blunt. For example, "because it pays more" is not a good answer. However, stating that, "The position offers more responsibility, challenges and interesting opportunities, as well as a higher salary," is a good answer.

Why do you want to work for this company?

Don't answer this question with, "Because you advertised for an X on Indeed.com." Your answer should offer what you think are the most interesting aspects of the company, for example, "because it is on the cutting edge of technology" or "because you are the industry leader." The research you do on the company in order to prepare for the interview should give you an answer to this question.

When can you start?

It is customary for most employee's to give at least two weeks notice to an employer. Those in management positions are expected to give longer notice. You will not earn points if you express disrespect toward your current employer by telling the interviewer that you plan to quit your present job without giving sufficient notice. He will assume you will show his company the same amount of disrespect. It is also a good idea to tell the interviewer you plan to start learning about your new position/employer on your off-hours (i.e., reading employee training manuals, etc.) Telling the interviewer you can't begin work for a few months because you want to take some time-off is not a good idea.

What is your commitment to this job?

Most people would respond with an answer avowing a deep commitment to the company and the job; however, a better answer would be to state that your commitment will grow as you get to know the company and the people in it.

Aren't you overqualified for this job?

Note that employers don't like to hire overqualified people because they won't stay around long. But since it is probably obvious that you're overqualified, admit that you are, but also emphasis the positive. For example, "I am overqualified in some ways. I have more experience that is required for this job, but you are looking for someone who is an expert in X, and that's me. However, that doesn't mean I'm completely overqualified. I feel that I have much to learn in the area of X, which is a big part of this job and I know it will keep me challenged...."

What salary are you expecting?

Don't sell yourself short when asking for a specific salary. Studies have found that those who negotiate for a higher salary often get it. You should do some research before the job interview so that you don't ask for too much or too little. You might be asked to justify why you are worth the salary you are asking, so be prepared with an answer (i.e., tell them how your skills and experience will benefit the company so much that your salary will be a bargain for them).

The best salary resource on the Internet is Salary.com where you can find out what people earn at various experience levels and in every region of the USA. At the time this was written, you could search the Salary.com database free. You also need to consider the cost of living in the area you will be relocating to, if applicable. There are cost of living calculators on the Internet. A good one can be found at Homefair.com. With a cost of living calculator, you can find out how much you will have to earn in your new location to maintain the same standard of living you enjoy in your present location.

A good answer: "After doing some research at Salary.com and a few other sites on the Internet, I am asking for a starting salary of $100,000. I base this figure on the fact that I have seven years of experience in the field and have proven myself to be a great asset to my past employer. I realize that this figure is $20,000 more than I am presently earning; however, the cost of living is considerably higher in the San Francisco area and I have included an amount to cover the higher costs I would have to pay if I relocated here."

Why should we pay you the salary you're requesting?
Answer this question by convincing the interviewer that you deserve the salary you're requesting. The best way to do this is to point out how you have benefited your past employers in terms of increasing profit, reducing expenses, improving efficiency, etc.

Good answer: "Last year I exceeded my annual sales quota by $500,000 and gross profit by 30 percent. I achieved over $3.5 million in sales in a two year period setting a company record for most new accounts created in one quarter. I intend to bring in much more each year for your company than I will earn. Therefore, I believe this is a fair salary."

Are you considering offers from other employers?
It is strongly recommended that you NOT disclose any offers you have received or discuss the companies with whom you have interviewed. A good answer to this

question is to state that you want to keep offers from other companies confidential. (Of course, if for some reason you believe you would have a better chance of getting the job offer if you disclosed this information, then do so.)

Do you have any questions?

This question is usually one of the last questions an interviewer will ask, as it is a logical way to end an interview. Never go to an interview without preparing questions to ask beforehand. Avoid asking about salary, vacation time, employee benefits, and such until you have asked a number of other questions that demonstrate your interest in working for the company. Good questions to ask the interviewer:

- Why is this position available?
- How do you measure performance and success in this position?
- What are your expectations for the first 30-60-90 days in this position?
- Is this a new position? How long has this position existed?
- How many people have held this position in the last two years?
- Who would be my supervisor? To whom would I report?
- Who will I supervise?
- With whom will I be working most closely?

- What do you like about working for this company?
- What are the current plans for expansion or cutbacks?
- What kind of turnover rate does the company have?
- How financially sound is this company?
- What projects and assignments will I be working on?
- What happened to the person that held this position before? Was he promoted or fired?
- What is this company's culture, (i.e., is it rigid and formal or relaxed and flexible)?
- What are the current problems facing the company (or my department)?
- What do you like the most about working for this company? The least?
- What is the philosophy of the company?
- What do you consider to be the company's strengths and weaknesses?
- What are the company's long and short term goals?
- Describe the work environment.
- What attracted you (the interviewer) to this organization?
- Why do you enjoy working for this company?
- Describe the typical responsibilities of the position.

- What are the most challenging aspects of the position?
- Describe the opportunities for training and professional development.
- Will I receive any formal training?
- What is the company's promotional policy?
- Are there opportunities for advancement within the organization?
- When can I expect to hear from you?
- Is there any reason why you can't offer me this position today?
- You can also ask questions regarding information you found when conducting research about the company.

Is there anything else about you I should know?

This question is usually one of the last asked. Don't answer with a simple, "No." Instead, use this question to try to get the job offer. You can do this by answering, "Yes, you should know that I really want this job. After talking with you today, I feel that this is a position that would provide me with lots of opportunities for career growth and advancement and I feel I could really contribute to this company. I have the business experience and ability you're looking for and the required management skills as well. Is there anything that prevents you from offering me this position today?"

What have you heard about our company that you don't like?

You will probably have to do research to answer this question, particularly if the company isn't well known and you haven't heard anything about the company. If you don't know of anything negative, then answer "I honestly haven't heard anything negative about your company. I did some research on your company before answering your online job posting and I didn't come across anything negative." If you have heard some bad news about the company, such as the fact that it is unstable or operating in the red, then say so, "I have heard that last year's profits were way down and I am concerned about this."

What aspect of this job appeals to you the least?

In asking this question, the interviewer is trying to determine if you dislike doing a major part of your job. For example, if you're a file clerk, you obviously don't want to answer by stating that you hate to file. Like most people, you probably hate doing the routine, boring administrative tasks that everyone has to do; therefore, you might want to answer accordingly, "I don't particularly like compiling the monthly sales reports. I love the sales process, meeting and negotiating with clients, and working in the field all day. Sitting in front of a computer for a few hours each month doesn't particularly appeal to me; however, I know it needs to be done, and I've always done this task as required in my previous jobs, but I don't particularly like doing it."

How will you handle the parts of this job you like the least?

This question is very similar to the previous question and should be answered positively, "I will perform all of the tasks my job requires on time and to the best of my ability regardless of whether or not I enjoy them."

What are you looking for in your next job?

A good way to answer this question is by expressing enthusiasm for the opportunity to grow and develop and be promoted to the next level. In addition, your answer should be relevant to the job you're seeking. A good answer: "In my current position, I have worked on numerous teams designing computer software products and on occasion have acted in the capacity of project manager. I am looking for a position where I can be project manager on a regular basis as I have excelled at doing that whenever I had the opportunity. I enjoy the process of leading the team, organizing and strategizing and managing the workflow in order to develop an effective product."

What did you do at your current (or last) job that increased profit, reduced expenses, or improved efficiency?

Sample answer 1: "I increased profit 30 percent my first year on the job by developing a new training program for the sales agents. Not only did sales increase, but employee turnover was cut in half."

Sample answer 2: "As file clerk, I was in charge of maintaining client records. The sales staff was having problems locating files when clients called in, so I reorganized the filing system and computerized it so that they could locate client files within 10 seconds without leaving their desks; this greatly improved efficiency."

Sample answer 3: "The restaurant was losing a large amount of inventory every year through employee theft, so I told the owner he should install a new security system. He took my advice and as a result employee theft was reduced significantly and the restaurant owner saved more than $30,000 the last three years in lost inventory. Also, the owner was losing money due to employees submitting fake orders. I recommended a computerized ticketing system that reduced employee theft to almost zero and increased profits by $10,000 last year."

Sample answer 4: "As secretary at Acme, it is my responsibility to make travel arrangements for all the executives in the office. I researched travel packages on the Internet and negotiated with several vendors for discounts and was able to save $18,000 last year in travel-related costs."

Do you know who our major competitors are?

You do not want to answer this question "No." In fact, being able to discuss who their competitors are in-depth can only help you get the job. You need to research this question before the interview and know who their top competitors are. A good answer: "Yes, your three major competitors are A, B, and C companies. Currently, you are the industry leader, however, B has plans to enter the X sector and challenge your dominance in this market." You might want to learn about each company's strengths and weaknesses as well. If they are publicly traded companies, you can learn more about them by examining their SEC papers.

For recent college graduates, you can expect a few questions along these lines.

Why did you decide to attend X college? Are you happy with your choice?

Always state that you are happy with your choice, even if you aren't. Do not state "it was the only place that would accept you." Do not make negative statements about the school or your professors. A good reason for choosing a particular school is that you liked the particular program they offered, or it is known for offering a good education in your particular major.

What factors did you consider in choosing your major?

The best answer is to state that you have always wanted to become X since you were a child and chose your major accordingly. If you're changing career fields or applying for a position unrelated to your major, tell the interviewer you were interested in that subject at the time, but circumstances have taken you down a new path.

Add a positive spin to it by stating that you have benefited tremendously by changing careers (learned new things, made you more hardworking, and so on).

What is your GPA? Do you feel it reflects your true abilities?

If your GPA is high, this question is easy answer, "My GPA is 3.8." If your GPA is not that good, perhaps you can make it better by calculating your GPA for the course work related to your major.

Good answer 1: "My overall GPA is not that good, 2.8; however, if you consider only my engineering course work, my GPA is 3.8. It was the required course work I had to take in English and Political Science that lowered my GPA . And no, my GPA isn't an accurate reflection of my abilities. I had to work part-time to support myself while attending college. I had a limited amount of study time and I thought it best to spend it on engineering subjects rather than Political Science and English."

Good answer 2: "My GPA was 2.9. I don't believe it is indicative of my true abilities, as I am capable of getting much better grades. In fact, in high school I had a 4.0 GPA and graduated in the top 10% of my class. I got a bit sidetracked my first year of college and spent too much time socializing and attending parties. However, if you look at my transcript, you will notice my grades significantly improved the last two years of college."

How has your schooling (internships) prepared you for this position?

Don't tell the interviewer that your schooling or internship has completely prepared you for the position, because it did not. Sample answer: "My internships have prepared me for this position in that they gave me basic real-world experience in the accounting field. The most important lesson my internships taught me is that the accounting skills I learned from college textbooks is not enough. The real world presents you with problems and situations not found in a textbook. My internships allowed me to significantly improve my skills in the areas of preparing monthly statements, handling accounts receivable and payable, and completing tax returns for small businesses, so I feel I'm a good candidate for this position as these tasks are a major part of this job."

If you had it to do over again, would you choose the same major?

Always say that you would choose the same major even if you wouldn't. If you don't, the interviewer might think you don't really know who you are or what you want, and consequently, might not be a very good worker or stay with the company very long. Good answer: "Yes, I would definitely choose the same major since I am very interested in computer science."

What was your favorite course in college and why?

Always answer this question with a serious course related to your major. Good answer: "I particularly enjoyed statistics, which might seem strange, since most people detest it. I think I liked it so much because I was particularly good at it. In fact, the professor asked me to tutor other students having difficulty with the course material."

How did your college experience change you?

Obviously, your college experience prepared you to enter the workforce, but what else does the interviewer want to hear? You emerged from your college experience more well rounded, introspective, hard-working, disciplined, mature, and so on. Good answer: "When I entered the university four years ago I thought I knew what to expect in college and what it meant to be a teacher. But two years into college, I began to appreciate the hard work and dedication required to be a good teacher. I think my college experience changed me in that I have great respect for teachers and the education industry than I did when I first entered college."

Do you intend to further your education?

Almost every job requires learning and improving, therefore, you don't want to give the impression that you don't like learning or improving by saying, "No, I'm through with school. I never want to sit in a classroom again!" Instead, it would be better if you state that you will be earning a degree, graduate degree, taking continuing education classes, etc., even if you aren't committed to furthering your education.

Good answer 1: "Yes, I have less than a year of school left to complete and I intend to enroll in a few classes each semester until I earn my degree."

Good answer 2: "Yes, I am always taking classes at the local college to keep current on the latest in computer programming. I'm also required to take a few classes each year to maintain my CPA certification."

Good answer 3: "Yes, I intend to eventually go back to school part-time to earn my master's degree in accounting. However, I want to take a year off and get settled in a new job and home before starting."

Why were your grades not very good in school?

There are several legitimate and believable answers to this question. One answer might be that you had to work full-time in order to support yourself. Another answer might be that you just aren't good at taking tests. In any event, if your grades were not that good, you're going to have to say something to overcome it. Don't blame it on others, such as your professors, who "were out to get you." Take responsibility for it: "I know my grades weren't that good in school, but I've never been very good at taking tests. I don't think my grades are an accurate reflection of my ability. I feel that I know this field as well as any new graduate. I just don't do well on tests."

If you only had bad grades in an unrelated field, then it shouldn't prevent you from getting the job offer: "I made

A's in engineering, but C's and D's in English literature classes I was required to take to earn my degree. I've just never enjoyed reading literature and poetry, so I wasn't particularly good at researching and writing the numerous papers that were required in these classes, so my grades were mediocre as a result."

Why didn't you participate in internship programs while in school?

Like many people, you probably had to work while attending school. If this is so, just answer with "I had to work full-time during school and wasn't able to participate in internship programs." Not all schools have enough internships available and perhaps one wasn't available. If so, a legitimate answer would be, "There weren't many internships available at Acme College as few employers in the area were willing to participate in them." If you made good grades and took a full class load, but didn't participate in internships, you might answer: "I thought it was best to take a full class load, concentrate exclusively on my studies and earn a high GPA rather than work part-time and let my studies suffer." In any event, don't leave the interviewer with the impression that you weren't motivated or were more interested in lounging by the pool than working when you weren't in school.

Why are you applying for a job unrelated to your internship experiences?

A good answer to this question is to state that your internship opportunities were not related to the career path you wanted to concentrate on and you took the internships just to get some experience in the field or that you learned from your internship experience that you liked a particular area of your chosen field.

Good answer 1: "There were a limited number of internships and I did not have the luxury of choosing from multiple options that matched my areas of interest. I thought it was best for me to get some experience in the field, even if it was in an area of accounting that didn't particularly interest me."

Good answer 2: " I thought I wanted to concentrate my career in tax accounting, but after working for several large CPA firms, I decided that I enjoy auditing much more than I do tax accounting and decided to pursue that particular area of accounting instead."

Why are you applying for a job not related to your degree?

This is a tricky question because you can't simply answer, "I decided after graduating that I don't like my degree choice and will work in another field instead." If you can't find a job in your chosen field and are interviewing for other jobs, then just say so: "As I'm sure you know, thousands of computer-related jobs have been outsourced to other countries and many of us have been left unemployed and unable to find work in the field. Therefore, I'm concentrating on finding a position that utilizes my accounting skills."

Of course, if you are a liberal arts graduate, chances are high you won't find a job that requires a degree in history, political science, English, etc., and so you have a good excuse: "I majored in history because I love the subject; however, there are few jobs that require a history degree. Like most liberal arts majors, I would probably have to earn a master's or a doctorate in history and get a teaching certificate in order to fully utilize my degree. I don't know if I will ever go back to school and earn an advanced degree, but in the meantime, I need to work and support myself.

What extracurricular activities did you participate in?

You want to come across as a well-rounded student, but not a party animal. Don't answer this question by saying you participated in numerous fraternity events. Instead, focus on extracurricular activities that had something to do with your major: "I participated in the Student Accounting Association. We met weekly, studied together, discussed accounting problems, held fundraising events and socialized. I was also a member of the University Student Computer Association. This year we won a region-wide contest in computer programming beating out 53 other university computer associations by creating a program that..."

For management level, you should expect questions like these;

Have you ever fired anyone?

The interviewer does not want you to express either too much indifference or too much sympathy for those you have had to fire. Tell the interviewer how you discussed the employee's shortcomings with him several times and tried to help him improve, but as a last resort, you had no choice but to fire the person.

How do you motivate employees?

There isn't a simple way to motivate all people due to the vast number of personality types and situations in which people work. The best answer is one that tells the interviewer that each employee must be uniquely motivated. You should offer several examples of situations where employees were successfully motivated.

What is your management philosophy?

Your management philosophy should be one that is fair and balanced, meaning that you are neither a dictator nor a pushover. Good answer: "I believe that a manager's job is to hire the best people, treat all workers fairly, motivate and give them all the resources to succeed, lead by example, and build a culture on open communication and worker satisfaction for an efficient and profitable company. And the success of a good manager is proactive in anticipating problems and being open to ideas and suggestions from employees for company growth and success. A good manager will always continue to work on professional growth and development."

What type of management style do you believe is most effective?

This question is similar to the above question and can be answered the same way. Generally, managers should not be dictators or pushovers. Sample answer: "I believe that a manager's job is to balance company goals with worker satisfaction in order to make the operation as efficient and profitable as possible. For example, a big part of Wal-Mart's success is the management philosophy of Sam Walton, who believed taking care of his employees was just as important as taking care of his customers. You don't see that much anymore, which is why so many companies are not nearly as profitable as they could be." Note that many companies do not place very much importance on employee satisfaction and therefore, the sample answer above might not get you the job. If you can, research a company before the interview to find out more about its culture in order to formulate an answer that will impress the interviewer.

What experiences have influenced your management style?

Tell the interviewer about a past experience or two that influenced the way you manage. Sample answer: "When I was an entry level manager at Acme, there was an extremely abrasive and rude executive who thoroughly intimidated his employees, and they, in turn, couldn't stand him. As a result, employee turnover was around 80 percent. The company spent a fortune hiring and firing new sales and marketing professionals, who were unmotivated to do a good job and lasted about a year before they became fed up with their tyrannical boss and resigned. As a result, our branch office was the lowest performing division in the country and I don't think the people at corporate headquarters ever understood why. This experience taught me that one must be approachable and listen to subordinates in order to be an effective manager. When I left Acme, and became CEO of XYZ Industries, I made sure that the sales and marketing staff were well trained and motivated, and felt free to come to me with their problems and suggestions. As a result, my division was ranked in the top 10 percent each year that I was CEO and employee turnover was extremely low."

Who have you patterned your management style after?

Think of a manager you have worked under or have learned about and tell the interviewer why you admire his or her management style. Good answer: "I patterned my management style after Frank Johnson, who was the CEO of Acme Corporation. I did so because he was the most effective manager I have ever known. His subordinates loved him, and worked hard for him. As a result, the company had a very low turnover rate and profits were very high. I think this was because the employees were so motivated to do a good job for him. He was very fair and friendly to the staff, but he wasn't a pushover. He required his employees to respect him, but they were not afraid to approach him and give input, and he would listen to them and adopt their suggestions most of the time. I was an entry level manager at the time and I decided back then I was going to adopt his management philosophy because I think it was why Acme was and still is the industry leader and considered to be one of the top companies to work for."

Some questions are considered illegal during an interview. Federal and state legislation prohibits employers from asking certain questions during the interview based on race, religion, creed, sex and age. Not all employers are familiar with these laws, particularly small employers. What should you do if you are asked illegal interview questions based on race, religion, creed, sex or age? I recommend that you very tactfully point out that the line of questioning is illegal.

Questions employer's are not supposed to ask job applicants:

- What was your maiden name?
- When were you born?
- When did you graduate from high school?
- What is your race?
- Do you have physical or mental disabilities?
- Do you have a drug or alcohol problem?
- Are you taking any prescription drugs?
- Would working on weekends conflict with your religion?
- What country are you a citizen of?

- Have you ever been arrested?
- What language did you speak in your home when you were growing up?

What should you do if asked an illegal question? It would be wise to point out to the interviewer that he has asked an illegal question. You can simply respond, "I'm sorry, but I don't feel that question is relevant to the position for which I'm interviewing."

Ending the Job Interview

If you're interested in the position, at the end of the interview, let the interviewer know this by stating (**ask for the job statement**): "I am excited and very interested in this position. Is there anything that prevents you from offering me the job right now?" When making this statement, say it with *enthusiasm* and *confidence*. Use that statement to close your job interviews and "ask for the job" (not in a desperate way). Always close an interview by "asking for the job."

CHAPTER 9
30 INTERVIEW QUESTIONS TO ASK IN AN INTERVIEW TO STANDOUT

At the close of an interview, when the interviewer says, "Do you have any questions?" always have questions to ask. Interviewers expect you to ask questions. An interview is a two-way conversation between the interviewee and interviewer. The interviewer is trying to determine if you are the best job candidate for the position and you are assessing whether the job and company are a good fit for you.

Stand out in your interview with hiring managers by having a list of insightful questions to ask. Prepare a list of 7-10 questions for your job interviews. Never go to an interview without questions to ask beforehand. Avoid asking about salary, vacation time, employee benefits, and such until you have asked questions that demonstrate your interest in working for the company. When asking questions, ask them with enthusiasm and a positive attitude.

Asking intelligent questions allows you to learn more about the position, challenges, opportunities, company and your boss. Your questions will also give you a chance to highlight your skills, knowledge, experience and help you stand out to the interviewer.

30 Smart Questions to Ask the Interviewer:

- Why is this position available?
- Can you describe the characteristics of someone who is successful in this role?
- Is this a newly created position?
- How long has this position existed?
- How many people have held this position in the last two years?
- Who would be my supervisor?
- Whom will I supervise?
- Who will I be working closely with?
- What do you like about working for this company?
- What are the current plans for expansion or cutbacks?
- What kind of turnover rate does the company have?
- What are the most important tasks I can help you accomplish within the first 90 days of employment?
- What projects and assignments will I be working on?
- What happened to the person that held this position before? Was he promoted or fired?
- What is this company's culture, (i.e., is it rigid and formal or relaxed and flexible?)
- What are the current problems facing the company (or my department)?

- What do you like the most about working for this company?
- What do you like the least about working for this company?
- What is the philosophy of the company?
- What do you consider to be the company's strengths and weaknesses?
- What are the company's long and short term goals?
- What attracted you (the interviewer) to this organization?
- Why do you enjoy working for this company?
- Describe the typical responsibilities of the position.
- How is performance measured in this role?
- What are the most challenging aspects of the position?
- Describe the opportunities for training and professional development.
- Will I receive any formal training?
- What is the company's promotional policy?
- Are there opportunities for advancement within the organization?
- When can I expect to hear from you?
- Is there any reason why you can't offer me this position today?

Always prepare a list of 7-10 insightful questions to ask the interviewer to stand out from the competition and leave a lasting first impression to get hired.

CHAPTER 10
HOW TO TURN A JOB INTERVIEW INTO A JOB OFFER-7 STEPS TO MAKE A CONNECTION AND GET HIRED

How do you make a lasting, memorable connection with someone? Empathize with them, work to uncover their pain (a problem they are currently experiencing), understand the problem, and propose a solution. Establish a connection that shows how you will add value to the individual's life.

What does this have to do with job interviews? You'd be surprised: Growing evidence suggests that making a memorable connection with a hiring manager—and the business they represent—is essential.

All too often, we leave our natural interpersonal skills and instincts at the door when we enter job interviews, assuming that professional interactions require a detached attitude. However, while it's true that professional conversations should be focused and structured, the principles that drive engagement are relatively universal. The key to turning a job interview into a job offer lies in making an emotional connection with the hiring manager, one that allows you to identify the business's "pain" (a problem the company urgently needs to address).

Step One: Understanding the Difference between Assets and Value

The majority of job candidates make the same mistake: They think that a hiring manager's top priority is to ask the question, **"Why should we hire you?"** To be more precise, they believe that a hiring manager wants to review the skills and experience (the assets) of each candidate. They think that a hiring manager's primary goal is to choose the candidate with the most experience and the highest number of relevant skills. They assume that the purpose of an interview is to verify the authenticity of the job candidate's claims and make sure they have an appropriate professional demeanor.

A hiring manager is ultimately looking for what sets you apart from other similarly qualified candidates, in other words, they want to see your *value*. Discovering this hinges on answering a different question altogether: **"What problem would hiring you solve?"**

While you can learn a lot about a person's history and skill level by reading through their resume, what you can't usually figure out "on paper" is how they think. After all, resumes and cover letters are often rewritten multiple times, sometimes with the aid of senior professionals and professional writers and editors. **When a hiring manager brings you into a real-time environment—the interview—they want to test your problem-solving skills.**

In an ideal world, the interviewer will have some excellent value-probing questions written and rehearsed, making this process clear-cut. However, we're not living in an ideal world, and more often than not the job candidate has to guide the value-sharing process; this is where having an established and practiced interview technique becomes vital: Interviewers often don't have much time (and patience) for the interview process. Conducting interviews takes precious minutes away from their usual duties and costs the company money.

The interviewer wants to know whether or not you can do the job well, and they want to know ASAP.

At the same time, however, hiring managers have been known to ask vague or off-beat questions that seem to have little to do with the offered position, e.g., "What would your former co-workers and ex-employees say about you?" When this happens, if you haven't prepared yourself adequately, it's easy to get thrown off balance. Tricky questions like these can cause you to misread the interviewer's needs and throw your focus off discovering the business's pain, resulting in a less memorable interview.

To avoid being thrown off task by tricky interview questions, rehearse for your interview efficiently. The interview advice presented herein will teach you how to stay on task and keep your eye on the prize.

Step Two: Understanding Business Pain

To discover a company's "business pain," you'll first need to have a complete and specific understanding of what business pain is, exactly. Ask probing questions that focus on uncovering the problems with the hiring manager or interviewers department. The goal of uncovering the hiring managers "business pain" is to make an emotional connection, by showing your problem-solving skills so that you stand out as a must hire candidate.

Step Three: Finding Business Pain with Probing Questions

Here are some questions to ask the hiring manager or interviewer to begin engaging them:

1. What are some of the problems your department faces right now?
2. What issues can be addressed in the next 30, 60 or 90 days?
3. What are some of the challenges in this position?
4. What do you want an employee to accomplish, in this position, in the first 90 days?
5. Can you tell me about the team I will be working with?
6. How would you describe the responsibilities of this position?
7. How would you describe a typical day in this position?
8. How would you describe your management style?

9. What is the key to success in this position?
10. How is success measured in this position by you?

Step Four: Selling Your Problem Solving Skills

Spontaneously demonstrating problem-solving abilities is a major stumbling block for many interview candidates. It's easy to create uncomfortable pauses while you stop to think, for example, or you may express your ideas in a vague or confusing manner without realizing it. Fortunately, there's a way to prepare for this stage of the interview with the STAR formula.

The STAR (Situation, Tasks, Action, and Results) formula provides a model for shaping your existing experiences into specific examples of when you solved problems similar to the ones the business is experiencing. The STAR formula can be broken down as follows:

- **Situation**: Think of a challenging situation you've encountered that you believe to be similar to the company's current difficulties. If you have never dealt with the exact issue the company is having, use the closest known equivalent or look for a situation you experienced in which you developed highly transferable skills.

- **Task**: What did you have to achieve to resolve the challenging situation, e.g., what task were you given and how did you complete it successfully despite the obstacles you encountered in the process? If you were not assigned a specific task and instead devised a course of action, you may wish to think of the "T" in STAR as "Target" rather than "Task." Your Target is the goal you set for yourself to resolve a challenging situation. Talk about how you concluded that the goal you selected was the right goal and describe how you achieved it.

- **Action**: As you talk about how you carried out your Task or achieved your Target goal, describe the specific steps you took. Vague examples like "I improved our marketing efforts" will not convey your real value; always talk about how you did things rather than just stating what you did.

- **Results**: Describe the outcome of your actions to the hiring manager. Once again, be as specific as possible, using hard data like facts and figures wherever possible (for instance, "I increased social media engagement by 30%, which drove a subsequent 15% increase in sales during the fourth quarter of 2015"). You should follow up by mentioning what you learned as a result of your experience and how you've implemented the skills you gained since.

The STAR formula may not be the best formula to use if your experience is based upon your ownership of a small business. If the STAR formula does not work for your experience, you can use the more straightforward PAR formula(Problem,Action,Results). The PAR formula requires that you recount a Problem, describe your Actions and discuss the Results.

Step Five: Building Emotional Trust as the "Must Hire."

As useful as the STAR formula is it is not a guarantee that you will gain the hiring manager's trust. If, for example, you try too hard to portray yourself as the one and only candidate who can magically solve all of the company's woes—the candidate who has "all of the answers"—the STAR formula may backfire on you. Candidates who do this come across as arrogant and even condescending, not to mention the fact that hiring managers are not naïve; they have probably interviewed dozens of candidates during their careers. By now, they know that candidates who seem too good to be true are probably less than genuine. Moreover, the moment you lose your credibility in this way, you've lost your shot at the job.

Step Six: Asking For the Job

A surprising number of candidates, once they realize their interview has gone well, feel such a wave of relief that they forget to cross the official finish line: They fail to ask for the job. Failure to ask for the job is a grave error because, if you do this, you risk looking less driven and less serious about the position than other candidates who directly ask for the job. Remember: It's not enough to be able to do the job; your hiring manager needs to know you want to do the job. They want to feel like your interview with them is not "just another interview" to you.

There is, of course, a certain finesse to asking for the job. If you look desperate, the hiring manager will immediately wonder why, and doubt will creep into the trust you just worked so hard to establish with them. Rather than coming right out and saying something like, "So, do I have the job?" or, "May I please have the job?" Try looking at the hiring manager in the eye while telling them that you'd love to work for their company. Follow your statement up with three or four concise reasons why you feel this way. For example, express your belief in the quality of the company's products or talk about your admiration for a key player's contributions to your industry. Whichever aspect you choose to highlight, be as specific as possible when you mention why you feel the way you do. If you come across like you're flattering the company solely for the sake of getting the job, your credibility will suffer.

Step Seven: Sending a Thank You Letter

A thank you letter is much more than just a polite formality—it's your final opportunity to emphasize your value before the interview process is officially over. For this reason, you should never, ever send a quick generic thank you letter.

A considerable amount of information tends to get "lost" during and after verbal conversations. For example, the hiring manager might have become distracted when you were delivering a vital point. Perhaps, right after the interview ended, there was a workplace crisis.

Maybe she was unusually tired that day after having interviewed several candidates in succession (this is typically the case with afternoon interviews). A thank you letter is your one chance to mitigate these risks and reiterate your value, so make it count.

Do not write a three-page transcript covering the entire interview—no one will have time to read it. Instead, choose three or four highlights that will affirm your position as an excellent and qualified problem solver. List these as bullet points while making sure that each point conveys a benefit you will add to the company (be sure to relate these benefits to solving the business pain). Like your resume, cover letter, and interview, your thank you letter should answer the ultimate question: "What problem would hiring you solve?" Keep your focus on the company—what's in it for the organization and the hiring manager—rather than describing your skills and competencies for the sake of making yourself look supremely qualified.

25 Brilliant Questions to Ask Interviewers or Hiring Managers

As you've seen in one of the steps outlined above, it is vital that you engage your interviewer with intelligent questions. We have compiled the following 25 questions you can ask the interviewer to keep them engaged.

1. *Have I answered all your questions?*

This question gives you the chance to touch on all essential aspects of your strengths which you may not have covered during the interview. It will also help to remove any doubt the interviewers may have about your competence and suitability for the job.

2. Describe a typical working day.

You find out the number of hours you'll be spending on the job if you eventually get it. It also shows the interviewer how eager you are to start work.

3. What do you enjoy about working here?

This question can help you establish an emotional connection with your interviewer which will differentiate you from other applicants. Asking this question will give you a good idea about the working condition of the organization.

4. How much are you willing to pay for the position?

At the final interview, you can be firm and go into specifics about the financial remuneration of the position. You can be resolute concerning what you want for the services you'll be rendering.

5. Why is this opening available?

If many people have shuffled through the position, you are applying for within the past three years, that speaks volumes about the kind of organization you are about to enter. However, if it's a position that is newly created, it goes to show that the company is growing.

6. Who are the people I'd be working with?

Asking this question leaves you with information regarding the organization's staff strength and turnover. A simple question like "How many new employees have you hired in the last year?" can give you the necessary information you need regarding the organization's turn-over.

7. Are there opportunities for me to progress in my career?

While sounding overambitious and presumptuous isn't a good thing, asking this question will be a good demonstration of your ambition and a willingness to be around to help the company grow for an extended period of time.

8. How do you see this company in a few years?

Show that you have an interest in the growth and goals of the company by asking this question. It also demonstrates commitment and provides information to your interviewers on your values and how your goals are in line with those of the organization.

9. What is your definition of success?

Having a rough idea of what the company values and the way and manner they provide feedback can give you an idea of the culture and traditions of the company you are about to join. Additionally, you can get a basic knowledge of your prospective boss and his views.

10. What's the next step?

Asking this question explains the process and lets you know when the company will likely contact you. Asking this question is a good way of showing confidence and a burning desire for the job.

11. Who do you think would be the ideal candidate for this position, and how do I compare?

To get some insight into whether you will get the job or not, ask the interviewer about his or her ideal candidate. It can also be of great use to you in preparing for future job searches and interviews. However, you have to be able to keep your composure in case the interviewer says something you do not like when it comes to comparing your performance to their ideal candidate.

12. Who would I be reporting to? Are those three people on the same team or different teams? What's the pecking order?

This question is meant to give you more knowledge about the job. It will help you understand the organizational structure of the team. If the proper description is given to you by the interviewer, you will have full knowledge of the people you are going to work with once hired.

13. Who do you consider your major competitors? How are you better?

Before asking this question, you must have a general idea of the major competitors of the company. You are likely going to find out more about the selling points of the company which the interviewer will highlight as things that made them better than their competitors.

14. Do you have any hesitations about my qualifications?

Think about this question as an honest assessment of your qualifications by the interviewer. Accept any hesitations mentioned without showing signs of dissatisfaction.

15. Can you give me an example of how I would collaborate with my manager?

Although this may look like being overly ambitious, it shows your readiness to work with your manager. This question gives you an opportunity to take note of a few of the things that will be required of you, if hired.

16. Can you tell me what steps need to be complete before your company can generate an offer?

An insight into this question will help you know if there are other things you need to do before you start work. It is essential to take note of the answers provided as you may have to refer back to them later.

17. What have past employees done to succeed in this position?

Asking this question may be pivotal to your success in the position and reveals your readiness to optimize your performance for the benefit of the company.

18. How do you help your team grow professionally?

Consider this as a way of knowing whether the company will be of benefit to your career or not. If there is no clear answer, it could be an indication that there is no help offered by the company to its team.

19. When your staff comes to you with conflicts, how do you respond?

Since conflict resolution is one of the critical parts of how a company manages its staff, knowing how those at the helm of affairs respond to conflicts is essential.

20. Will I have an opportunity to meet those who will be part of my staff/my manager during the interview process?

While this may sound unnecessary, the answer may help you prepare for the evaluation of your potential co-workers.

21. I read X about your CEO in Y magazine. Can you tell me more about this?

Without a doubt, this question reveals that you have been following the progress of the company for a while. It is even capable of increasing your odds of getting the job.

22. What's your staff turnover rate and what are you doing to reduce it?

This question can help you decide whether the job is worth it or not. It might also give you an idea of the level of satisfaction employees derive from working at the company.

23. Is there anyone else I need to meet with? Is there anyone else you would like me to meet?

Whether a superior or colleague, there may be someone else you need to meet before getting the job, so don't hesitate to ask this question. If possible, ask about the relevance of the person to your chances of being hired.

24. How would you score the company on living up to its core values? What's the one thing you're working to improve?

Every company has its core values; hence, you should ask about the efforts of the company towards achieving these values and improving them.

25. Beyond the hard skills required to perform this job successfully, what soft skills would serve the company and position best?

Knowing the soft skills that suit the company and position can help you improve yourself to perform more effectively.

If you follow the seven steps in this chapter, your odds of turning your next interview into a job offer will increase significantly. Keep in mind, however, that if by some chance you don't get the job, there's another useful step you can take: Phone the company and politely ask why you didn't get hired. Hiring managers are often surprisingly willing to tell you which skill they felt you were lacking (as long as you're respectful) allowing you to use unsuccessful interviews as a form of career guidance. Experience is, after all, the best teacher: Learn from it, combine it with the correct techniques, and keep practicing until you master the interview process. While it's a lot of hard work, the job you get will ultimately be more than worth it.

CHAPTER 11
HOW TO CREATE A 30-60-90 DAY EMPLOYMENT ACTION PLAN THAT WILL IMPRESS ANY HIRING MANAGER

Taking a 30-60-90 day employment action plan to a job interview will impress hiring managers.

It is not wise going into any job interview without a 90-day plan for how you are going to attack the job.

A 30-60-90 day plan demonstrates four things to the hiring manager:

It shows that you understand the job. You can't even begin to create this kind of a plan without knowing what you're doing.

It shows you can do the job. Based on how you talk about your plan, it conveys to the hiring manager your strategic thinking skills and other thought-processes that relate to your success on the job. The hiring manager is going to hear that you understand the job, you've performed similar activities, and that you know what it takes to be successful.

It shows that you will do the job. Because you're willing to create a plan like this, you demonstrate that you're willing to go the extra mile to get the job done.

It shows the hiring manager that if they hire you, it won't be detrimental to their own continued employment. It dramatically lowers the risk factor for hiring you. The way you communicate this is to use this plan to show them how you'll be successful in the role.

That's why a plan like this works so well for every job. It shows the hiring manager that you know the job, that you'll be able to hit the ground running, and that you know what it takes to succeed-which makes their job easier.

Starting a new job comes with a multitude of emotions, some good and some bad. Fortunately, the wonders of organization come to the rescue, yet again, as the transition is eased through the 30/60/90-day plan.

An unfamiliar routine, or lack of a routine altogether, can cause for added stress as well as the growing pressures to impress and succeed at the new position. Although your stress may build for a variety of reasons, getting organized always alleviates the nervous tension at the core of getting started.

A plan of any sort provides us with a tangible version of where we are going and where we want to be, all while tracking our progress and achievements along the way. By planning out your goals of the first 30, 60, and 90 days on the job, you have created your own vision and you are sure to take advantage of your full potential as a new hire.

In just a small timeframe, you are expected to learn how to do your job successfully, in addition to discovering how to fit in. Your 30/60/90 day game plan can get you there. Here is a sample outline of suggested goals to incorporate into your own, customized plan:

30 days – The Learning Stage

One common mistake of new hires is never taking the time to understand precisely what the company is trying to accomplish through their strategic plan. As a new hire, it is incredibly important to put in the effort to study and learn the internal lay of the land as follows:

- Bring the mission statement and vision to life and discover the plans the company abides by to reach these core values.
- Understand your boss's expectations of you.
- Begin forming professional relationships with coworkers.
- Learn about your customers and clients.
- Investigate the overall company culture.

60 days – Adding the Y-O-U

Once you have taken time to fully assess the company, begin adding your strengths to the equation:

Progressively begin building your own personal brand within the company by showcasing what you do well.

Brainstorm the ways in which your personal touch can accelerate company growth.

You may have started with listening much more than talking, which is recommended. By this stage, begin leveling out the playing fields by contributing to the conversation.

Furthermore, be an effective communicator by being open. You're the newbie but don't hide behind your computer screen two months in.

Become more versatile by taking on some tasks outside of your set responsibilities.

Continue to be mindful of your boss's expectations of you.

90 days – The Transformation Stage

By this time, you should have a firm grasp of the role you play in the company. Your confidence is likely to have grown since your first day and your leadership qualities are hopefully itching to be put to action. At this point, consider the following:

- You know your employer well enough by now to be proactive when it comes to company happenings.
- Be attentive and aware of new projects and come ready with possible solutions.

- Analyze the growth in your network.
- Avoid novice mistakes.
- Look into broadening your horizons by getting more involved. You can do this by joining a club, council, board, or committee.
- Make time to acknowledge your growth and reward yourself for your progress.
- Your 30/60/90 day plan is your written path from a new hire to an effective leader. By organizing and prioritizing, you can make the most out of the initial stages of your new job.

Job Seeker's Guide To Creating A 30-60-90-Day Plan

The first 90 days in a new job typically sets the tone for your employment. Three months is the standard "grace period" for new employees, how you handle those first weeks and months on the job is critical.

Creating a 30-60-90 day plan as part of the job interview process can not only help you win the job offer, but it can help guide your actions during the transition period for your new position. The plan is a written outline of the strategy and goals you have for the first three months in a new position. It demonstrates an understanding of what the job involves and your ability to perform the job.

Developing a 30-60-90 day plan requires that you prepare yourself mentally for a new position by planning the activities and projects that will help you learn what you need to know about your potential new employer and co-workers while setting yourself up for success in the first 90 days on the job.

You can develop a 30-60-90 day plan for almost any position, but they are most commonly used in sales, management, technical, and administrative jobs. In certain types of positions — for example, sales or sales management jobs — you may actually be asked to create a 30-60-90-Day plan as part of the interview process. However, taking the initiative to create a plan — even without being asked — can set you apart from other candidates and demonstrate your understanding of the role and qualifications to handle the challenges the position offers.

Creating a plan sends a signal to the hiring manager that you are a serious candidate and that you are willing to invest the time and resources necessary to be successful in the position. It can demonstrate your knowledge of the company's needs and outline the skills and abilities you'll put into action to effectively perform in the position. It distinguishes you from other candidates for the position by focusing on the company's needs and requirements and showing how you can make an immediate impact in your first 90 days on the job. The 30-60-90-Day plan can enhance your chances for receiving an additional interview and secure the job offer. Once you are hired, the plan can serve as a roadmap for success in your first 90 days in your new position.

Your 30-60-90-Day plan will address many aspects of business matters, including products, customers, technologies, company culture/politics, and strategies.

After 90 days in a new position, your supervisor expects you to be making an impact in that position. The 30-60-90 day plan helps ensure you'll achieve this goal.

Important Note: In developing the 30-60-90 day plan — especially in the execution phase — focus on what, not how. That is, identify broad targets, but don't provide detailed specifics on how you plan to implement each task, thereby creating a document that could be used as a roadmap by another candidate or by the company itself if you're not offered the job.

Outcomes should focus on solving problems for the company (i.e., retaining customers, increasing revenue, fixing specific problems) or capitalizing on opportunities (increasing sales, expanding the business, attracting new customers, being more competitive).

When to Develop the 30-60-90-Day Plan

Generally, there are two specific time periods when you might develop your 30-60-90 day plan. The first could be after your initial job interview, when you've started identifying how you can be a fit for the company's needs. You might actually suggest to the hiring manager at the end of the interview that you create a 30-60-90 day plan so that he or she can assess whether you'd be a good fit for the organization. In securing permission to create the plan, you may request permission to conduct informational interviews with people you'd be working with in the position. This is an opportunity to get to know your future co-workers and obtain information that isn't available through third-party research alone. Your request to create a plan indicates serious interest in the position.

The second timeframe for creating a 30-60-90 day plan is after the second or third interview but before a hiring decision has been made. It's sometimes at this point that the hiring manager request you create a plan, instead of you taking the initiative to create one. Some experts recommend waiting until this time to create a plan, because you'll know more about the company and the job than you might after the first interview.

Where to Get the Information for Your 30-60-90-Day Plan

This document can set you apart from other candidates by demonstrating an understanding of the role and a specific plan for meeting the company's needs. Of course, to create the document, you must have information about the company, the job, and the industry. You can gather this information by researching the company and industry, its customers, conversations with your job interviewer, future co-workers, supervisors, and vendors serving the company or the industry.

Here are some of the sources you can consult for research:

- The job description/job posting for the position
- The company's website (including news releases, mission statements, and the company's annual report)
- The company's social media channels (Twitter, Facebook, LinkedIn, YouTube, etc.)
- Third-party websites like GlassDoor.com (www.glassdoor.com) or WetFeet.com (www.wetfeet.com) allow you to read the opinions of former employees
- Media coverage (trade journals as well as mainstream media coverage)
- Google
- Ask the hiring manager to provide you with access to additional data that will help you develop, i.e., financial and operating reports, strategic and functional plans, employee surveys, etc. (Keep in mind, the company may not want to provide you with this data unless you are hired, so you may not have access to this information until you're an employee.)
- If you know someone who works for the company — or if you can network your way to be able to talk to a current employee — you can ask them questions to assess the current situation
- You can also talk to people who are currently working in the field to gain a better understanding of the job, company, and/or industry

One of the best sources of information is your interview with the hiring manager for the job.

Listen carefully for information that relates to the organization's strategy, technical capabilities, corporate culture, and organizational politics. During the interview, pay careful attention to spot clues to the hiring manager's problems and concerns and identify the company's plans for future growth.

Here are some questions to ask in the interview that will help you prepare the plan:

- What is the biggest challenge facing the organization in the next six months or year?
- How is this role expected to address the challenge facing the company? (Or is it?)
- What does he or she absolutely need you to accomplish within the first 90 days?
- What would he or she like you to do beyond that during the first 90 days?
- What is the most promising — yet unexploited — opportunity for growth? Why isn't the company pursuing that opportunity right now?
- What is the biggest problem you need solved by (this job title)?
- Is this position focused on new projects, turnarounds/realignments, or sustaining success?

Take a few moments after the interview and write down everything you can think of that relates to:

- Problems the hiring manager and/or company is facing

- Opportunities that haven't yet been pursued but that are a priority

- Your personal weaknesses/shortcomings that may need to be addressed in follow-up communications to strengthen your position as a candidate

Formatting Your 30-60-90-Day Plan

The typical 30-60-90 day plan is a Microsoft Word document with 1-5 pages — or a PowerPoint document with 7-12 pages — that is usually sent electronically to the hiring manager, either after an interview or before a follow-up interview.

In each 30-day period, you want to focus on 3-7 initiatives or projects. Trying to do too much will be counter-productive. It's very easy to take on too much during your transition into a new position, but you can't achieve results without focus. Identify the most high-value activities and prioritize those in your plan.

You can use the template below to create your 30-60-90 day plan, customizing the initiatives to the specific company you're targeting. The plan needs to speak to the hiring manager's needs and the company's specific challenges and opportunities. A generic plan will not be effective.

Template for a 30-60-90-Day Plan
Introduction/Cover Letter

The introduction provides an overview of what you would like to accomplish in the first three months on the job. Outline specific outcomes you'd like to achieve at the end of the first 90 days.

In the introduction, provide a disclaimer that the plan is provided to stimulate communication about the company's specific needs in this role and how you, the candidate, can hit the ground running to meet those needs. State, however, that the plan is subject to revision in collaboration with the supervisor's specific needs.

Be as specific as possible, however, you will want to leave open the possibility that these tasks can be amended or modified if desired, in consultation with the supervisor.

The body of the plan is divided into three separate content sections: the first 30 days, days 31-60, and days 61-90. Each section contains specific tasks or initiatives.

First 30 Days (Meet/Learn/Understand)

In the first 30 days, your goal is to analyze your situation and ensure the priorities you focus on in the next 60 days are ones that will get you started on the right path. Understanding the history of the organization and learning organizational dynamics and structure will help you recognize potential pitfalls and challenges due to company culture and/or internal politics. You will use this time to meet key internal personnel and external stakeholders, educate yourself about the company and its products and services, get to know your co-workers and customers, and collect the information that you will need in order to plan and execute the projects you'll be working on. A large part of your work in the first 30 days is to learn about the organization's history and culture.

However, there is a balance between learning and doing. Spend too little time learning, and you may make decisions that alienate your new colleagues. Spend too much time learning, and your supervisor may wonder if you will accomplish what he or she wants you to do in your new role.

During this time, your activities may focus heavily on building relationships, getting advice, and gathering information. It may seem strange to focus time and attention on these activities, but the information-gathering and learning phase is important. You must identify people in the organization who have the information you need and begin to build relationships with them so you can learn from them. At the same time, don't neglect taking action on small projects that can build positive momentum.

Sample objectives:

- Meet with the supervisor to identify specific short-and long-term project goals and key initiatives.

- Make a list of co-workers and schedule informal lunches and meetings with key team members, colleagues, internal stakeholders, and management to identify important issues, discuss past successes, form relationships, and assess company culture.

- Identify who else in the company you need to meet. Ask your supervisor for a list of the ten key people outside your department that you should get to know, and then set up meetings with those people.

- Are there external relationships you need to build (i.e., customers or vendors?). Research the needs of current customers and analyze existing company relationships with customers. Meet with all existing account contacts.

- Complete company training and/or self-learning to get up to speed on products, services, policies, procedures, and company culture.

- Are there are any other shortcomings in your learning you need to address (i.e., training on a specific software platform)?

- Research existing company literature (website, mission statement, employee handbook, newsletter/daily email list, etc.)

- Review competitive opportunities and create a report to establish closable business in the next 60 days, 90 days, and six months.

Remember, you will want to choose no more than 3-7 initiatives per 30-day period.

Days 31-60 (Strategize/Plan)

Once you have taken time to assess the company and get up to speed, the next 30 days will focus on planning and strategizing. What shortcomings can you help address? Your efforts in the first 30 days are focused on building credibility — but the next 60 days emphasize strategizing and planning to improve performance.

You will also start to learn "how things get done" in the organization. You must sort out who does what, the roles of each individual and department, and how the group has worked together in the past. You'll want to plan how to create internal and external networks — "coalitions" — to get things done. Who do you need support from in order to achieve change? Don't neglect "influencers" — people outside your direct chain of command who have the power to make things happen. Sooner or later, you'll need the support of people over whom you have no direct authority. During this 30-day period, figure out who those people are and how to work with them.

Action is also important in the 31-to-60-day timeframe. Show how you can take what you've learned and apply it towards accomplishing specific tasks or projects. You will begin to demonstrate how you can contribute to achieving the company's goals.

One of the items to include in this time period is a review of the plan with your supervisor to clarify mutual expectations and assess progress toward the plan completion. Now is the time to make course corrections, especially as it relates to the execution phase of the plan.

Sample objectives:

- Meet with supervisor to assess progress in first 30 days and determine priorities and plan adjustments for next 60 days.
- Ensure all plans for first 30 days are completed.
- Continue to have bi-weekly meetings with team members to move forward on [XYZ] project.
- Create territory routing and call cycle plans to increase the number of contacts with existing accounts.
- Develop an account prospect database (compiled from Hoovers, trade journals, LinkedIn, Salesforce.com, and incoming leads).
- From discussions with the supervisor and product specialists, formulate a plan to close short-term opportunities.
- Meet with key account decision-makers and identify specific steps needed to bring in business this year.

- Schedule four new account meetings per week. Update the CRM weekly to grow the prospect database.

- Create a pilot program for [a specific new initiative] and gather team and client feedback.

- Begin to strategize on a major initiative to focus on in the final 30-day period of your 30-60-90 day plan.

Days 61-90 (Execute)

In the final 30 days, you will focus on execution. In this time period, make sure you are concentrating on initiatives that matter to your boss. Identify what your supervisor cares about the most and try to create results in those areas. It's essential to focus on executing one or more key items that your supervisor has outlined. In other words, your efforts during this time should be consistent with achieving one or more of your supervisor's top business priorities.

In the final 30 days, begin to demonstrate how you can move from being reactive to proactive. Be aware of new projects being developed and be ready to contribute to the conversation and planning process. Look for opportunities to become more connected by participating in an internal committee, cross-functional task force, or professional association. These will keep you on the cutting edge of what is happening in your specific role, at the company, and in the industry as a whole.

You'll also identify long-term goals and begin strategizing how to accomplish those plans beyond your first 90 days.

Sample objectives:

- Meet to assess your first 90 days and develop a plan for the next 90 days and the rest of the first year in your new position.

- Exceed monthly sales quotas by increasing the level of contacts with key accounts. Assess where the company stands as a vendor of choice with accounts and whether the customer has the ability to make the purchase in the next six months. Identify any roadblocks to making the sale.

- Continue to network with successful Account Executives throughout the company to identify best practices for lead conversion and making the sale. Set up monthly conference calls to share ideas for making contacts and closing sales.

- Develop a two-year plan to dramatically increase market share and make the company the vendor of choice for the top 10 prospect accounts.

Outcomes

In the first 90 days, you aren't just learning — you're expected to contribute as well. You want your supervisor, co-workers, and colleagues to see an immediate impact. Part of this is identifying those tasks that can lead to "small wins." Achieving these outcomes in the first 90 days builds momentum and increases your visibility and credibility.

By the end of your first three months in your new role, you want your supervisor, your colleagues, and your subordinates to see the impact you have made on the organization. Small, early wins can create energy and forward progress.

Call to Action

At the end of the plan, suggest the next step. If you've had one interview, you might suggest meeting for a second time to review the plan and assess whether the priorities you've identified would meet the company's business objectives. If you've had several interviews, you might reiterate your serious interest in the position and your desire to be the one to execute the plan.

This may seem extremely straightforward and bold, but you've now invested quite a bit of time and energy in identifying the company's needs and problems and developing a plan to address how you can solve them, so asking for the opportunity to execute on the plan is simply following through.

Even after you've presented the plan to the hiring manager, it's not complete. You might learn additional information in further interviews that would change your initiatives.

Of course, once you've gotten the job offer and secured agreement from your supervisor for your 30-60-90 day plan, you have a game plan to guide your first 90 days in your new job.

CHAPTER 12
TIPS ON HOW TO SUCCESSFULLY CLOSE
AN INTERVIEW AND FOLLOW-UP

Knowing how to successfully close an interview can make the difference between getting the job and being one of the unfortunate individuals who receives a rejection letter in the mail. While much attention is given to the matters of how to write a resume and cover letter as well as what to expect in regard to interview questions, far too many job seekers are unprepared when it comes to knowing how to successfully close an interview. Keep in mind that this is perhaps your last opportunity to demonstrate why you are perfect for the job. Successfully closing an interview walks a fine line between being too aggressive and not being aggressive enough.

Always ask for the job in every job interview. Look the hiring manager in the eye and tell him or her that you want to work for them and then tell them why. Show your enthusiasm and give a strong summary of the *value* that you will bring to the company as an employee.

It's always a good idea to have 7 to 10 insightful questions that you can ask the interviewer at the end of the interview. This shows that you have more than just a passing interest in the position and truly want the job. If you have taken the time to do your research on the company, this also demonstrates initiative and increases your chances of being hired.

Once all questions have been asked and answered, it is quite appropriate to ask the interviewer when they anticipate making a hiring decision as well as what the next step in the interview or hiring process will be. Make a point to ask the employer for a business card so that you can have readily available contact information to follow up with the employer in the days to come; this will also make it easier for you to mail the all important interview thank-you letter as soon as you return home. The thank you letter must show the "value" you will bring to the company and your enthusiasm for the job position. Never send out a generic thank you letter.

Also don't forget to shake hands with the employer and summarize how your skills and experience, as well as ambition and desire, make you the perfect candidate for the position. If you're really confident and don't mind taking risks, you might ask "So, is there anything stopping you from offering me the job right now?" This ploy should only be used if you feel the interview has gone well, however. Otherwise you might be setting yourself, as well as the interviewer, up for an embarrassing response.

A softer version of this tactic would be to ask, "Is there anything else I can answer for you to make a hiring decision?" If you really aren't sure how well the interview went and don't want to waste your time waiting for a call that may never come, you could ask, "Have I done well enough to advance to the next level of the hiring process?"

Asking if you've done well enough to advance to the next level in the hiring process puts all the cards on the table and an employer who appreciates honesty and frankness will reciprocate by telling you where you stand. If you are not the candidate, the employer was looking for, asking this question might give you a golden opportunity to clear up something that might make you the ideal candidate. Otherwise, at the very least, you won't be spending the next two weeks waiting by the phone and you can begin concentrating on other employment prospects.

In the event that the employer does not offer you a firm commitment and seems to be a bit hesitant about when a decision will be made, don't take it as a personal affront. There could be any number of reasons why the employer is reluctant to hire you on the spot-the least of which could be the need to consult with superiors. It's important to remember if you are disappointed about not receiving a job offer on the spot, that you remain positive, upbeat and confident. Finally, take time to thank the employer for meeting with you. Above all, remember to always be professional no matter what happens.

CONCLUSION

Successful job interviewing is more critical today than in recent times. It is the single most important test that differentiates between receiving a job offer or not. It is not unlike an actor's audition for a role in a movie. You have one chance to pass the test. Yet, many people think they can adlib the job interview with off-the-cuff, unprepared, and unplanned answers. This impromptu behavior is one of the surest ways to leave empty handed. Here are the essentials of job interviewing.

Plan. This means think things through ahead of time, what you are going to say and how you are going to say it. Think about how you intend to dress for your job interview. You can predict what questions are to be asked during a job interview, so think about how you intend to answer them.

Organize your thoughts about your answers and prepare a few questions to ask the interviewer. Arrange your ideas ahead of time, think of possible questions you might be asked, be able to support your opinions, bring samples of work, offer specific accomplishments that have relevance to the organization, and identify a final question. Organizing your ideas and resources the proper way increases your odds of having a successful interview.

Practice some of your main points out loud to hear the sound of your voice, this is an example of role-playing, either by yourself or in front of someone else. When you hear your voice before the interview you are less apt to be surprised by what you say and how you sound. However, don't memorize answers or questions because you are likely to come across as rigid and mechanical.

Keep your posture erect but relaxed during the face-to-face interview. This means sitting at the edge of the chair, not leaning all the way back in the chair. Sitting at the edge of the chair keeps your body and mind more alert and shows off your attention and interest towards the interviewer.

Smile at the right times to support your points. Look friendly and approachable. You want the interviewer to view you as someone she can trust and would want to work around.

Look directly at the interviewer without staring or gaping. Nod "yes" when agreeing but avoid nodding "no" when disagreeing. Avoid anything that suggests negativism. If you disagree, then say you disagree, or say you have another idea.

Refrain from awkward body movements. While you might be nervous during the interview, you want to appear to be in control. So, make your body movements smooth, and even. Make your voice work for you. While you might not think you have a good sounding voice; it is what it is. You can take voice lessons, but there are basic tenets to using your voice to work for you. For example, avoid monotone, avoid speaking too fast or too slow, and avoid speaking too loud or too soft. Practicing your answers aloud, as suggested in item 3, helps voice control.

Articulate clearly and use words that are appropriate for the level of the job and terminology used in the profession. You want to appear as someone "in the know," so you need to use the "language" for your career job. Otherwise, you are apt to be viewed as a "outsider."

Listen carefully to the questions asked, and answer the questions directly, honestly, and completely. Do not offer a response to a question that has not been asked, stay focused.

As mentioned previously, the interview is a test. The test consists of two parts: how qualified you might be for the job, and how unqualified you might be for the job. Some interviewers focus on qualifying you, while some interviewers focus on disqualifying you. Most interviewers consider both parts. What this means for you is that you must carefully prepare well before you go for an interview.

Ace your job interviews and get hired!

ABOUT THE AUTHOR

Robert Moment is The Get Hired Expert, Interview Coach, Speaker, and Author.Robert specializes in interview coaching that helps ambitious professionals stand out in job interviews, get hired and make more money.

Contact Email:
TheGetHiredExpertRobert@Gmail.com

Visit:
www.HowtoAceanInterview.com

Robert Moment is the author of the following best-selling books:

- Resume Writing-How to Write a Resume With Examples That Will Make You Stand Out and Get Hired
- Cover Letter Writing- How to Write a Cover Letter That Will Land You a Job Interview to Get Hired
- How to Prepare for an Interview
- What to Wear to an Interview
- Interview Questions and Answers-100 Interview Preparation Questions to Stand Out and Ace Your Job Interview to Get Hired

CPSIA information can be obtained
at www.ICGtesting.com
Printed in the USA
FSHW021642140219
55681FS